John Truscott

D0173461

OPERATION
BISMARCK SEA

LAWRENCE CORTESI

MAJOR BOOKS • CANOGA PARK, CALIFORNIA

Copyright © 1977 by Lawrence Cortesi

MAJOR BOOKS
21335 Roscoe Boulevard
Canoga Park, California 91304

All Rights Reserved.

No portion of this book may be reproduced in any
form without permission in writing from the publisher,
except by a reviewer who may quote brief passages
as a part of his review.

PRINTED IN THE UNITED STATES OF AMERICA

ISBN 0-89041-156-5

**Library of Congress
Catalog Card Number: 77-70375**

CONTENTS

ACKNOWLEDGMENTS

For their assistance in providing material and advice in the preparation of this book, sincere thanks to the Department of the Air Force; Lt. Col. C.B. Kelly, III, Chief, Secretary of the Air Force, Office of Information, Los Angeles; and Mrs. Joan F. Osako, Chief, Public Information, Los Angeles.

FOREWORD

The Bismarck Sea operation proved to be the most important achievement for American air power since its inception as a combat weapon. It was the first time that aircraft, operating from land bases and without naval support, had attacked and destroyed a naval armada on the open seas. Until this battle, the worth of air power had always ignited controversy among military leaders. The most outspoken of the advocates for an air force independent of other branches of the armed forces, like General Billy Mitchell, often suffered persecution by textbook strategists who considered air power a mere supporting arm for other military departments.

At best, the air corps had been designated an auxiliary force to support ground troop operations, amphibious landing operations, or tactical operations to disrupt enemy supplies and communications. In fact, all of the warring nations of World War II had initially considered air power a support element for ground forces and navy surface forces. While squadrons of aircraft often sank a surface ship, no air unit without supporting surface warships had ever engaged an armada as large as the 22 ships of the Lae Resupply Convoy in Operation Bismarck Sea. Fifth Air Force planes *alone* engaged the enemy armada and air power *alone* assumed the responsibility for stopping the powerful Japanese fleet of surface ships. Only if the Fifth Air Force succeeded could air power win its place as a military arm that equalled or surpassed other types of combat forces.

Operation Bismarck Sea offered Fifth Air Force an opportunity to prove the worth of air power. However, the operation blew hot and cold over a hectic three-day period and the fight was not decided until the final hours.

And, regarding the Bismarck Sea action, the reader should understand the controversy over the makeup of the Japanese Lae Resupply Convoy.

All official reports from Southwest Pacific Headquarters in Brisbane, Australia, and from Fifth Air Force ADVON Headquarters in Port Moresby, New Guinea, indicated the Lae Resupply Convoy included 22 ships: two cruisers, eight destroyers, six troop transports, four freighters, and two tankers. The reports of the convoy's complement were established by reports from PBY and P-40 reconnaissance pilots as well as from combat airmen who attacked the convoy over the two-day period, March 2-3, 1943. As late as 1948, General Douglas MacArthur, commander in chief of Allied Southwest Pacific Forces, and General George Kenney, commander of Far East Air Forces, insisted that the reports of Allied airmen were accurate and that the Lae Resupply Convoy did indeed consist of 22 ships, including ten warships.

Yet, three noted World War II historians, Samuel Morison, W. F. Craven, and J. L. Cate, concluded that the Lae Resupply Convoy only included sixteen vessels: eight destroyers and eight transports. They based these conclusions on Japanese documents on the Bismarck Sea action captured at Goodenough Island and on ATIS (Allied Translator and Interpreter Section) reports from several Japanese officers involved in the battle. On the basis of these interview reports, the three historians claimed that transports *Kamo Maru* and *Shichisei Maru* (which turned out to be freighters and not troop transports) were not part of the convoy. They also claimed that some of the destroyers were counted twice because they had hurried to Lae after the attack to discharge Japanese survivors and then returned to the scene of action.

These historians further claimed that no cruisers were involved; that the *Shirayuki* was merely an oversized destroyer and not a cruiser; and that the cruiser *Tenryu* had been sunk two months earlier by American submarines and could not have been part of the Lae Resupply Convoy. However, the Fifth Air Force also claimed they had sunk the *Tenryu* off Madang in January, 1943.

Interpreters who interviewed hundreds of Japanese after the war said that Japanese officers rarely admitted the extent of their losses (nor did most ex-United States officers for that matter). Further, Fifth Air Force intelligence officers who interviewed captured Japanese service troops at Hollandia in 1944 were told that the cruiser *Tenryu* had only been damaged by submarines and air force planes in early 1943. The cruiser was lost in the Bismarck Sea operation. Further, these same prisoners said that Admiral Masatomi Kimura, whom they called the Eel of the Pacific, always carried his flag aboard a cruiser, a fact nobody denied during the entire Solomon campaign. Even later in the Leyte operations, he directed his flag from a cruiser. It would seem odd that Kimura would carry his flag aboard a destroyer in this single Lae Resupply Convoy operation.

Finally, to deny that freighters and tankers were involved in the Lae Resupply Convoy is astonishing. Fifth Air Force photographers took several photos of skip bomb attacks on freighters, including the freighters *Kamo Maru* and *Shichisei Maru*. Also, experienced Fifth Air Force airmen could certainly recognize freighters and tankers when they saw them.

These historians did admit that a later document, Supplemental Order #57, contained the names of some vessels that were not on the original #157 order.

Thus, in piecing together reports from all sources, the Lae Resupply Convoy that left Rabaul on February 28, 1943, appeared to have had the following complement of vessels: cruisers *Shirayuki* and *Tenryu;* destroyers *Arishio, Tokitsukaze, Asashio, Yukikaze, Uranami, Shikanami, Hatsayuki,* and *Asagumo;* troop transport *Marus: Nojima, Kyoikuse, Oigawa, Teiyo, Nichieyu,* and *Myoko;* freighter

Marus: Shichisei, Kamo, Gisha, and *Kembu;* and two un-named tankers.

In truth, it really doesn't matter how many ships made up the Lae Resupply Convoy. The success or failure of Operation Bismarck Sea would have produced the same results: a vital test for air power, the future course of the Southwest Pacific war and, of immediate importance, the sparing of Australia from Japanese invasion. But for the sake of story continuity, this book relates the strange World War II battle on the basis of a 22-ship convoy.

L. Cortesi

Chapter One

THE CANCER OF WAU

Wau is a mile-square patch of kunai grass deep in New Guinea's Owen Stanley Mountain Range. It is a most unlikely focal point for the Southwest Pacific's most decisive engagement of World War II. Yet, this remote allied base, not even a dot on the huge, dinosaur-shaped island of New Guinea, triggered the crucial Operation Bismarck Sea. In turn, fickle Mother Nature toyed with frail humans as the Olympic gods toyed with the frail mortals of ancient Greece to decide the outcome of this strange battle between machines of the air and machines of the sea.

The tropical island of New Guinea itself, 3,000 square miles of dense mountain jungles, was a most horrible place for a war. Besides jungles and mountains, the huge island included primitive natives still living in the stone age, countless streams and swamps, an almost unbearable humid climate, and every conceivable type of insect and tropical disease.

"It must have been an angry God who made this place," an Australian medical officer once said of the island.

He must have been correct, because up to 1943 there had been only one serious campaign between Japanese and Allied ground forces—the Buna Campaign. The engagement had left both sides totally spent, for the mountainous, jungle island had riddled both sides with disease that far surpassed battle casualties.

Within a year after Pearl Harbor, Japanese armies had rolled through the Far East. In quick, multiple thrusts, Japan overran Korea, Southeast Asia, and the Philippines. Her navy, while the American navy lay half-shattered in Pearl Harbor, had easily supported amphibious landings on key islands in the Western and Central Pacific. Finally, Japanese ground troops had occupied Java and the Solomon Islands.

In the late spring of 1942, Japanese troops began the occupation of New Guinea and started the climb over the Owen Stanley Range. By summer, the Japanese Eighteenth Army, following the Salamaua Trail from Buna on the northern coast, had reached Kokoda. They were now only fifty miles from Port Moresby, the last obstacle to an invasion of Australia.

In the sweep over the Owen Stanleys, General Hatazo Adachi, commander of the Japanese Eighteenth Army in New Guinea, had elected to bypass the small Australian outpost at Wau, about 100 air miles west of Kokoda. When staff officers reminded Adachi that a contingent of Australians occupied Wau, the Japanese commander had only shrugged. "Wau is of no consequence. What will they do when we have occupied all of New Guinea?"

General Hitoshi Imamura, commander-in-chief of all Eighth Area Japanese forces in the Southwest Pacific, agreed with his Eighteenth Army commander. He said from his Rabaul headquarters: "It would be useless to expend time and troops on this insignificant Australian camp. We must occupy Port Moresby with minimum delay."

Neither Imamura nor Adachi anticipated any real problem in capturing all of New Guinea. They knew the Allies were already evacuating planes, men, supplies, and important papers from Port Moresby. Japanese intelligence had already informed General Adachi that General Douglas MacArthur, commander-in-chief of the Allied forces in the Southwest Pacific, was fortifying the Brisbane Line for a defense of Australia. So MacArthur was not only conceding the loss of New Guinea, but the loss of northern Australia as far south as Brisbane on the east coast.

But, an unforeseen move by the American navy brought a turnabout in the Japanese drive towards Port Moresby. In August of 1942, U. S. Marines landed on Guadalcanal in the Solomon Islands.

General Douglas MacArthur had been bitterly opposed to the Solomons landing. "The fate of Australia is at stake, and you foolishly expend men, planes, and naval units on a worthless island in the Solomons."

MacArthur reminded the Joint Chiefs of Staff in Washington that the Japanese enjoyed superior naval and air forces. They would not only destroy a Guadalcanal landing but their superior forces would decimate the depleted American naval units who tried to maintain the Guadalcanal beachhead. But, naval leaders had more influence than General MacArthur, perhaps because President Franklin Delano Roosevelt, an ex-navy secretary, favored the navy. Admiral Chester Nimitz got his way and the Guadalcanal landings went ahead.

MacArthur's predictions proved accurate. The Ironbottom Strait in the Solomon Islands chain became the graveyard of American warships. The U. S. Navy lost almost every naval engagement against the Japanese in a series of sea fights that followed the Guadalcanal landings. Further, because of frequent Japanese air raids, most of them only weakly contested, months passed before Henderson Field became operational for American aircraft. In fact, on several occasions there was talk of abandoning the Guadalcanal beachhead.

Yet, ironically, the Guadalcanal landings not only eased the immediate threat to Australia, but gave MacArthur a chance to strike back. General Hitoshi Imamura, from his stronghold in Rabaul, decided to shift men, planes, and naval forces from the New Guinea area to the Solomons area to oust the American marines from the Solomons. He considered the Guadalcanal landings a malignant tumor in Japanese-held territories. The shift of effort to the Solomons thus deprived the Eighteenth Army in New Guinea of logistics support and General Adachi was forced to postpone his drive on Port Moresby. His troops stood pat in their jungle camps at Kokoda, high in the Owen Stanleys.

The temporary suspension of Japanese operations in New Guinea gave Douglas MacArthur time to send his newly arrived 32nd and 41st Infantry Divisions into New Guinea to support the exhausted, disease-riddled Australian 9th Division who alone had withstood the entire Eighteenth Army. MacArthur also had time to base a pair of newly arrived air groups in Port Moresby, the 3rd Bomb Group and the 49th Fighter Group. The ground and air units soon launched a full-scale attack on the Japanese at Kokoda and forced them to withdraw northward to Buna. The Allied troops, with continued air support, chased the Japanese out of Buna and General Adachi evacuated his troops to Lae, 200 miles up the coast.

A wide length of dense, impenetrable jungle now separated the Allied Forces at Buna from the Japanese forces at Lae. Both sides were exhausted and disease ridden after the Buna Campaign, and neither side could muster the strength to launch an offensive against the other. But, in the process of evacuating eastern New Guinea, the "insignificant" camp at Wau soon posed a threat to the Japanese since it lay only 50 air miles from Lae, while more than 145 air miles from Buna or Port Moresby. And since the stalemate now settled to an exchange of air raids, Wau offered an advantage to the Fifth Air Force.

The American Fifth Air Force quickly took advantage of Wau and changed the quiet highland base into a busy staging area for American and Australian aircraft. They built a new 3,000-yard airstrip for emergency landings or for staging purposes before continuing on to bomb Lae, Madang, or Wewak. Fifth Air Force also constructed service and repair facilities to care for aircraft who made emergency landings after raids on Japanese bases. They built a strong line of bunkers on the western lateral of Wau to prevent any Japanese ground attacks.

The Japanese grumbled at what now had become an ulcer at Wau, but they did little else. Instead, during the next two-month lull in any ground wars, Japanese troops rested in Lae and Salamaua to recuperate from the hard Buna campaign. Similarly, the disease-ridden American and Australian ground units rested at Buna and Oro Bay. Only the air units of both sides were active, conducting sorties against each other on a somewhat irregular basis.

MEANWHILE, THE MILITARY LEADERS of both sides found time to plan new offensive strategies: General Hitoshi Imamura from his headquarters in Rabaul, New Britain, and General Douglas MacArthur from his headquarters in Brisbane, Australia.

MacArthur and his staff planned a new offensive called Operation Elkton. Under the plan, Allied ground forces would strike northward up the coast of New Guinea with amphibious landings against Lae and Madang. Once these were captured, the United States Fifth Air Force could move its aircraft 200 miles north, well within striking distance of strong Japanese bases in Wewak and the Admiralties, as well as the stronghold of Rabaul in New Britain. The Allies would reduce these bases, capture them, and reopen the road to a reconquest of the Philippines. However, to initiate the plan, General MacArthur would need several more divisions of ground troops, at least a dozen more groups of fighter planes and bombers, and all-out support from the United States Navy. He had little chance of getting much, since most of the Allied effort was in Europe.

At Rabaul, General Hitoshi Imamura had grown impatient with the ground war lull. He met frequently with his Eighth Area staff to draw up strategy for new offensives against Allied forces. "We must strike now," Imamura told his staff, "before the Allies can reinforce their exhausted army and depleted air force."

Imamura and his staff devised an offensive plan called Operation 157. The Japanese would reinforce the tired Eighteenth Army in New Guinea with fresh troops and plenty of guns, ammunition, and other supplies. They would send more squadrons of Zero fighters and Betty bombers to their bases in Madang, Wewak, and Lae to support the ground troops in a new offensive. This time, the troops would not plod over the jungle trails to Buna as they had earlier in the war. They would advance directly over the jungle trails to Kokoda again. Here, they would group for an assault on Port Moresby.

For the most part, only airmen and service troops occupied Port Moresby and they would be no match for the hard, determined jungle fighters of the Japanese Eighteenth

Army. Once they captured Port Moresby, the Japanese would effectively cut the Allied troops and air wings in Buna and Tufi. These troops would then have to abandon these bases or surrender. And, once the Japanese occupied all of New Guinea, they would use Port Moresby for a staging area for an invasion of Australia, only 100 miles south across the Coral Sea.

There was one key difference between the Allied dreams and the Japanese dreams. The Japanese had the resources to carry out their plan. General Imamura commanded a dozen well-trained combat divisions in Rabaul. They were fresh, eager troops who far outnumbered the exhausted three divisions of Allied troops in New Guinea. And, General Imamura could scatter more than 500 aircraft throughout the Japanese bases in Rabaul, Cape Gloucester, Gasmata, Wewak, Madang, and Lae. The American Fifth Air Force could only muster about 200 planes from its six air groups and one squadron based in New Guinea. But worse, because of excessive use, the Fifth Air Force could seldom count on more than a third of their aircraft for immediate combat. Too many planes were badly in need of repair and maintenance.

Finally, except for the Bloody Friday the 13th fight, the Japanese navy had decidedly trounced the American navy in the series of sea clashes in the Solomon Islands. The American navy, thus pummeled at almost every turn since the August landings at Guadalcanal, now remained squeamishly out of battle range, except in dire necessities.

So, while MacArthur waited futilely for reinforcements that never came so he could launch Operation Elkton, General Imamura, in January of 1943, signaled the start of Operation 157.

To test the Fifth Air Force, General Imamura sent a small convoy from Rabaul to Lae, a convoy that included only three transports and four escorting destroyers. If the convoy could successfully defy American air or naval strikes, Imamura would send the main convoy, with thousands of men and tons of supplies and equipment into Lae. American reconnaissance planes soon spotted the small convoy, and before long a dozen B-17's of the 43rd American Bombardment Group attacked the convoy from high altitude. But the Japanese helmsmen easily avoided the bombs. Later, a dozen medium bombers from the 3rd and 38th Bomb Groups attacked the convoy with about a dozen escorting fighters. However, they only scored a few minor hits before a squadron of Japanese fighters drove them off. The Fifth Air Force simply lacked the numerical strength to repulse the convoy.

On January 9, 1943, the Japanese convoy reached Lae with no losses. The ships disembarked the 102nd Japanese Brigade, 4,000 fresh troops. General Imamura's suspicion that the American air force was too weak to materially hurt the Japanese seemed accurate.

General Hatazo Adachi warmly welcomed the new arrivals to Lae. Adachi was even more eager than Imamura in Rabaul and he did not want to wait for the arrival of a second, much larger convoy from Rabaul. He asked Toru Okabe, the commander of the newly arrived 102nd Brigade, if he would initiate Operation 157 at once by capturing Wau. Okabe responded enthusiastically. He had suffered defeat at Guadalcanal and nothing could please him more than an opportunity to amend this disgrace with a victory in New Guinea.

"Wau is a cancer," General Adachi said, an ironic turn-around for a man who once called Wau a camp of no consequence. "We must dislodge the Australian Kanga Force from Wau and thus deprive the enemy of using Wau for staging his aircraft against us. And when we ourselves occupy Wau, we may use this base as a staging area for a push over the mountains into Port Moresby."

"It will be done," General Toru Okabe assured Adachi.

But, the Wau base would be no easy objective. Jagged slopes rose into gray tertiary rock on all sides of the mile-square plateau. In some areas, the walls were precipitous cliffs of harsh slate, some as high as two thousand feet straight up. Only from the west was the isolated mountain base accessible by foot traffic—winding uphill trails from Lae and Salamaua. But the trails skirted brush-covered ridges or wound through dense green foliage under the roof of high pocoduras and eucalyptus trees. The trails often were booby-trapped with poisonous plants, or poisonous snakes, or knife-sharp rattan burrs. And there were always the isolated bands of Watabi headhunters, the most primitive creatures on earth.

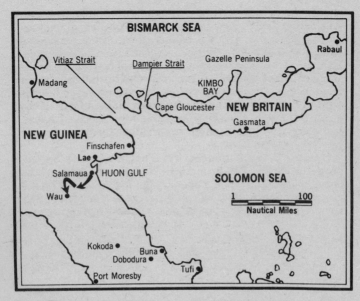

Map 1: The 102nd Brigade marches on the Kanga Force at Wau.

During the 1930s, Wau had been a jungle boom town after a Newcastle, Australia, adventurer had discovered gold in one of the Mambare ridges that surrounded Wau. Gold seekers climbed the trails and built thatched and canvas huts on the Kunai Mesa. Mining companies constructed metal buildings. But the gold rush vanished as quickly as it started and thick underbrush reclaimed the trails and flats around Wau. Not until 1941, after the bombing of Pearl Harbor, did white men come here again. A token Australian force came to Wau to build a small airstrip so that men could be ferried in and out of Wau by air. The Australian garrison here was called the Kanga Force because their own egress and ingress to Wau was to hop in and out by air.

Now, after the Owen Stanley fight, the Fifth Air Force had made certain that Wau was well defended to protect the newly built service and repair facilities for their aircraft.

However, the Kanga Force felt quite secure. Since the Japanese had ignored Wau during the aborted sweep over the Owen Stanleys the previous summer, the small Australian detachment at Wau, about 200 men, did not expect any current assaults against them. They considered their day-after-day vigil a monotonous, useless watch. Except for the occasional staccato hoots of bowerbirds or the shrill chirps of white-eyed sunbirds atop the tall eucalyptus trees, the Australians never heard anything in the jungles west of the airfield. The gloomy green maze in front of the defense bunkers, disappearing into a mysterious darkness, had become an object of curiosity rather than fear for the Kanga Force sentinels.

However, the Japanese were not dissuaded by the dangerous uphill jungle climb to Wau, nor by the reported new defenses at Wau. On January 25, 1943, General Okabe ate an early breakfast in his quarters at Salamaua with General Adachi. The Japanese commander of the Eighteenth Army had come down from his headquarters in Lae to offer an encouraging sendoff on the mission to Wau.

"May the gods go with you," Adachi told Okabe.

"I'm sure they will," General Okabe answered his superior.

AT 0700 HOURS, 1500 MEN OF THE 102nd Brigade, weighted down with dismantled mortars, small artillery, ammunition, and other supplies, left the coastal hamlet of Salamaua. For five days they plodded over the precipitous jungle trail towards Wau. By late afternoon of January 28, the advance patrols of the 1500-man force could see the clearings of Wau through the thick Eucalyptus trees. General Okabe, confident of an easy victory, told his men to bivouac for the night. They would strike in the morning against the unsuspecting Kanga Force.

However, if Japanese intelligence had been remarkably accurate, so too had been Allied intelligence. Besides Australian coast and jungle watchers, the Papuan natives of eastern New Guinea showed strong loyalty to the Australians who had ruled Papua in eastern New Guinea under a League of Nations mandate since the end of World War I. The Papuans, who lived a step above the stone age, had felt an immediate animosity towards the Japanese when their troops had invaded New Guinea nearly a year ago. The Japanese had often put the natives into labor, building airstrips, roads, and dock facilities, or forcing the natives to supply food for Imperial troops. The Papuans resented this treatment, and they willingly kept Australian authorities well informed of Japanese movements.

General Okabe had barely left the Salamaua outpost with his 1500 men when Papuan runners scooted over jungle trails to report the Japanese movement. Fully two days before Okabe reached the jungle mesa before Wau, the Australians knew the attack was coming and they knew the actual strength of Okabe's force.

Every Allied troop carrier that could fly was pressed into service. C-47 carrier planes ferried into Wau the 17th Australian Brigade along with supplies, ammunition, and two 75MM cannons. Accustomed to operating in tight places in New Guinea, the adept transport pilots landed 194 planeloads of 2,000 men and a million pounds of supplies on the 3,000-foot runway.

On the morning of January 29, General Okabe opened the engagement with heavy mortar attacks. However, the Australians were expecting the attack and they were well dug in. Thus, when the Japanese troops swarmed out of the gloomy forests and attacked the dugouts at the western end of the airstrip, the Australian 17th Brigade was ready. The Aussies countered with a blistering volley of rifle and machine gun fire, plus murderous point-blank fire from their two 75MM cannons. After a mere five minutes, the Japanese troops withdrew into the jungle, leaving a hundred dead and wounded on the kunai fields before the defense bunkers.

Okabe was astonished. How did they know he was coming? He sent out scouts to reconnoiter and they returned to tell him the Australians had perhaps one to two thousand troops dug in around Wau. General Okabe grimaced but he would not withdraw. He knew now that a frontal assault would be futile against so many men so he decided to employ infiltration tactics. Dozens of determined 102nd Brigade troops, alone or in pairs, wriggled stealthily through the thick brush or kunai grass to snipe away at Australian defenders, particularly those in the dugouts. The infiltrators caused only minor harassment in daylight, but what would happen with nighttime infiltrators?

The Australians, despite exposure to sniper and grenade

fire, were forced to employ new tactics of their own. They called on flame throwers and soon, squads of Aussies, dodging enemy sniper fire, sprayed swaths of oily flames through the kunai fields and acacia brush. The tactic worked and once more the Japanese disappeared into the gloomy forests.

But late in the afternoon of the 29th, the invaders struck again. *"Banzai! Banzai!"*

This time the emotionally charged troops of General Okabe swarmed out of the trees with reckless determination. Despite heavy losses, they overwhelmed the Aussie defenders on their initial assault and occupied one end of the airstrip. Here, despite heavy Australian fire, they set up mortar and artillery to begin an all-out fight for the airstrip.

It was obvious the Australian 17th Brigade needed help. The Wau commander radioed Buna. "Redwing under heavy attack; need air support. Repeat: heavy enemy ground attack; Redwing needs air support."

Buna was a half hour away by air and it would take considerable time to preflight and load attack planes to come to Wau's rescue. Fortunately, two squadrons of planes from the 49th Fighter Group had been on their way up the coast to conduct sortie attacks against Japanese activities in Salamaua. The planes were quickly diverted to Wau. Within a half hour, a squadron of P-38's and a squadron of P-40's, napalm bombs under the wings, approached Wau. General Okabe's assault troops had barely begun to construct their trenches when Okabe noticed that the Australians, instead of meeting the Japanese challenge, had retreated to the far end of the airstrip.

The Japanese commander soon understood why when he heard the whine of aircraft echo from the south. A moment later, the P-38's and P-40's loomed out of the Mambare ridges and skimmed over the airfield. First, the planes murderously strafed the Japanese troops at the far end of the strip. Then the Lightnings and Warhawks unleashed deadly napalm bombs over the Japanese positions. Once again, Okabe's 102nd Brigade sought refuge in the gloomy jungles. By dusk, the Australians had counted 250 Japanese dead.

But the determined General Okabe had not yet given up. He spent the night of January 29-30 licking his wounds and planning another assault in the morning. However, the Fifth Air Force had also spent a busy night—loading napalm bombs in the bellies of the 3rd Bomb Group's B-25's and their A-20 light bombers.

At the first break of dawn, three understrengthed squadrons, about twenty planes, skimmed over the patch of gloomy forest west of Wau. For a half hour they saturated the greenery with napalm bombs until a massive billow of sickening oily smoke darkened the early-morning sky. By 0600, not even the sounds of familiar bower birds echoed from the charred forest.

At late morning, elements of the Australian 17th Brigade moved cautiously into the blackened forest. They found dozens of burned bodies and tons of scorched supplies. However, the Aussies found no trace of General Okabe and the bulk of the 102nd Brigade. Okabe had apparently salvaged most of his men and was now on his way back to Salamaua. Wau thus remained in Allied hands—at least for the moment.

In Salamaua, General Okabe sadly recounted his unsuccessful assault on Wau. Strangely, General Adachi seemed more elated than disappointed. "We are far from lost," he told General Okabe. "The Buna struggle has left our enemy spent. They used every resource at their command to repulse less than half a brigade. And only through good fortune could they send aircraft to harass you at a most inopportune moment. Okabe-*san*, they could not stop your voyage to Lae a few weeks ago. And now," Adachi gestured, "they could only mount 12 fighters and 20 bombers to stop us at Wau. For days they flew soldiers into Wau, as our intelligence has since learned. But they could only muster 2,000 fighting men on the battlefield, barely exceeding in number your own small force."

General Okabe nodded.

"But for us, 50,000 eager sons of Japan wait at Rabaul," Adachi continued. "Five-hundred aircraft rest on our bases throughout the Bismarck Archipelago. Our staff waits impatiently to launch Operation 157. Your foray merely proves we have the overwhelming strength to do so." Adachi gestured again, emphatically this time. "We will strike again, more heavily and they will be too weak to hold this cancer at Wau. They will be too weak to stop us anywhere and we shall drive the Allies out of New Guinea."

General Okabe listened, encouraged.

"Even now," Adachi said, "I have been accorded an audience with the Honorable Imamura at Rabaul. He most of all is eager to push forth Operation 157."

Thus did the minor skirmish at the highland base of Wau set the stage for one of World War II's strangest confrontations: The Battle of the Bismarck Sea.

Chapter Two

PAPPY GUNN'S SKIP BOMB

Port Moresby was the final Allied deterrent to Japan's southern thrust through the Western Pacific. The base offered the only harbor in eastern New Guinea capable of sheltering a fleet. The area, a narrow coastal plain, protected the sea approaches to the north from the Coral Sea and it also anchored the maze of trails running over the Owen Stanley Mountains to the northern coast. The Allies had improved the harbor, built several airstrips, constructed dispersal areas and established an array of repair and service facilities. Its main airstrip, Eight-Mile Drome, could accommodate the biggest bombers. Further, tons of war materiel were stashed in the grass shacks and quonset huts under the jungle trees surrounding the base.

Allied submarines often staged from Port Moresby before fanning into the Bismarck Archipelago against Japanese shipping. Heavy and medium bombers in Australia, far out of range of enemy bombers, once staged here before going on to attack Japanese bases in the same archipelago. And from Port Moresby, the Allies relayed men, supplies, and ammunition to their ground forces in Buna, Wau, Oro Bay, and the Solomons. Finally, it was from this stronghold that the Allies had twice frustrated the Japanese drive towards Australia, once in the Battle of the Coral Sea and again in the more recent Kokoda-Buna campaign.

Inevitably, therefore, it was Port Moresby that became the vital objective for Japan's Operation 157.

At the far end of Eight-Mile Drome, three men stood on the shoreline and stared out at Merrick Bay where several sunken ships lay resting in the water. In a short while, modified B-25's would be circling and skimming towards these ships to test a new bombing technique.

Among the trio were Brigadier General Ennis Whitehead, deputy Fifth Air Force commander and commander of the advanced echelon of Fifth Air Force in New Guinea; Colonel Paul "Pappy" Gunn, head of the Fifth Air Force Service Command; and Major Ed Larner, C/O of the 90th Bomb Squadron, 3rd Bomb Group (L). All three officers would play a major role in Operation Bismarck Sea. And more important, the soon-to-be-tested bombing technique would become a crucial factor in the upcoming clash.

General Whitehead had developed an irascible and impetuous nature during his thirty years of service in the Army Air Corps, mostly because he resented the backseat designation for the air corps in the army's scheme of things. Even though the air corps was no longer in disrepute, Whitehead still spoke in sharp, rasping tones, whether he scolded a subordinate or whether he argued with a superior. He rarely relaxed. Instead, he constantly mulled over ways and means to improve air combat efficiency. No one around the stocky, round-faced general escaped his wrath if he failed to produce results.

Whitehead had begun his career in World War I where he had distinguished himself as a pursuit plane pilot. By 1920 he had risen to the rank of Major, but he almost ruined his career when he strongly supported General Billy Mitchell, the outspoken air power pioneer who aroused the army chiefs of staff by calling them criminals for turning their backs on air power.

When Billy Mitchell died in 1936, Whitehead had vowed to vindicate the air power pioneer. In 1940, Whitehead was assigned to the Far East Air Force, then based in the

Philippines. And, in early 1942, when the Fifth Air Force was established, Ennis Whitehead was promoted to Brigadier and placed in command of the advanced echelon of Fifth Air Force in New Guinea. Both General MacArthur and General Kenney, commander of the Fifth Air Force, apparently felt that Whitehead's ability as a combat tactician far outweighed his argumentive nature.

Now, at this threatened base of Port Moresby, Whitehead shuffled about impatiently at the edge of Eight-Mile Drome, waiting for the Merrick Bay tests.

Colonel Paul Pappy Gunn, formerly director of the Philippine Airline, had a lifetime in aircraft engineering. In February, 1942, he was awarded a field commission of Captain in the U. S. Army Air Forces and placed in charge of the old FEAF air transport command. Then, with only a few obsolete B-18's and C-39's, he successfully directed the evacuation of air corps personnel from the Philippines and from Java. He was then promoted to Lieutenant Colonel and placed in charge of aircraft maintenance of the newly created Fifth Air Force, established in the fall of 1942.

As director of the dilapidated planes of the old Philippine Airline, Gunn had learned every technique to keep unworthy planes in airworthy condition. He applied this knowledge to his new job as head of the Fifth Air Force Service Command and almost immediately he won a reputation as a great improviser.

During 1942 and early 1943, the Fifth Air Force had few serviceable aircraft and even fewer repair and service facilities, as against the numerically superior Japanese air force. But, despite the odds and 88 air raids on Port Moresby, Gunn managed to keep airborne the motley array of damaged, overworked, and outmoded planes. But more so, Pappy Gunn had successfully introduced improvised techniques that compensated for the lamentable state of the Southwest Pacific air arm.

No one knew the certainty of General Hatazo Adachi's threats more than Colonel Pappy Gunn, often called the "Mad Professor" by Fifth Air Force personnel. Gunn's imaginative mind had devised the parachute frag bomb for low-level attack by medium bombers, the 50-caliber nose guns on B-25's to make them support planes, and the napalm bombs to attack an unseen jungle enemy with flaming fire and smoke. Only yesterday at Wau, the attack on General Okabe's jungle-hidden brigade had shown the worth of one of these three techniques.

Now, the barrel-shaped Gunn was working on his latest experiment—a delayed fuse bomb that exploded eleven seconds after its release from a plane or five seconds after contact with a target. The fuse bomb was deliberately designed for the skimming B-25's and A-20's so they could hit surface ships with maximum payloads at minimum distance with perfect accuracy. The belated fuse would enable the pilot to get right on top of his target.

Pappy Gunn had asked Ed Larner and his crews of the 90th Squadron to test this latest technique in air-to-water surface attack. The colonel had selected some sunken hulks in Merrick Bay, outside of Port Moresby, as simulated targets: a freighter, two destroyers, and three transports. The derelicts had lain at rest in the shallow water for nearly a year, their superstructures protruding above the surface like a forest of stripped branches. For these many months, the array of scuttled vessels had reminded the Allied troops in Port Moresby of Japan's devastating air power.

In March, 1942, during the height of Japan's Kokoda offensive, Dina and Betty bombers had smashed the convoy's attempt to reinforce Port Moresby. Luckily, the holocaust occurred in shallow water, and most of the Australian soldiers and sailors had been rescued. But, the desperately needed supplies had been lost.

Nobody was sure the skip bomb would work. No crew member liked the idea of dropping a 500-pound bomb within twenty-five yards of a target. Nonetheless, one day after the successful air attack on Wau, Major Ed Larner and his crews would experiment over Merrick Bay.

Larner had agreed to the tests because he had long ago learned to respect the Mad Professor. Larner's own 90th Squadron pilots had put to use many of Gunn's innovations: changing B-25 medium bombers to low-level attack planes, reconnaissance planes, strafers, or frag bombers—a variety of functions what would have required several different types of aircraft.

"This skip bomb might solve our problem against Japanese surface ships," Gunn told Larner. "And, of course, since you fellows of the 3rd Bomb Group have had more experience in New Guinea than anyone else, I'd like you and your pilots to test this new technique."

So, the lean, oval-faced Larner had greeted Pappy Gunn's proposal with enthusiasm. If it could offer the slightest advantage over the Japanese, it would be worth it.

Larner understood too well the two elements in the Southwest Pacific that had frustrated Fifth Air Force attempts to stop Japanese shipping. First, there was the fickle weather in the Southwest Pacific where thick thunder clouds could jell in minutes to hide potential targets against medium bombers and high-level bombers. It was a sudden change in weather that had hampered the B-17 effort against the convoy carrying the Japanese 102nd Brigade to Lae several weeks ago. Secondly, the Japanese helmsmen had mastered the art of avoiding low-level torpedo and strafing attacks from fighter planes and low-level light bombers.

Nothing was more discouraging than the open defiance of Japanese ships of the Fifth Air Force, nothing more frustrating than the disembarkment of men and supplies on Japanese bases. The Tokyo Express in the Solomon Islands, where enemy convoys came down the Slot from Rabaul to deliver men and supplies to Guadalcanal, was an excellent example of Japanese contempt for the United States Air Force. Perhaps this skip bomb could exert maximum damage on Japanese shipping, despite the fickle weather or the adept Japanese helmsmen.

AT MIDMORNING, FEBRUARY 1, 1943, Larner and his 90th Squadron airmen boarded their aircraft at Eight-Mile Drome. Soon, the B-25's were circling like giant hawks over Merrick Bay.

With Larner in his plane, *Spook*, was his copilot, Lt. Sal Dineo, a young, nervous newcomer to the Southwest Pacific. The 23-year-old lieutenant had not yet acclimated himself to the harsh, jungle terrain over which he flew. On his first mission, to Lae, he had seen a B-25 go down and he wondered how, if by some miracle the airmen had escaped the plane, they could ever survive in the jungle.

Dineo sat stiffly in his co-pilot's seat when Major Larner straightened the B-25 only 20 feet above the water and roared towards the rusting freighter. Dineo could feel his nerves tingle as the bomber raced towards the sunken hulk.

And, as the plane approached the simulated target, the young lieutenant arched his spine and slammed it against the backrest of his copilot's seat, trying to restrain the hull looming before the nose of the B-25.

Sergeant Joe Cardis, the plane's gunner, was the third and last member of the modified B-25. He watched in awe from his bubble turret on top of the fuselage. Cardis had flown fifteen missions over Japanese bases in New Guinea and he too knew the potential fate of an airman who might parachute from a downed aircraft—death in the hostile jungle or in an uncharted patch of sea. In his bubble seat he licked his lips anxiously and then stiffened as the simulated target in Merrick Bay charged towards them. But a feverish curiosity co-mingled with the anxiety in his lively gray eyes.

Inside the pilot's cabin, as Lt. Dineo continued to ogle at the target, fear tore at his ribs and doubt rattled his mind. Suppose the bomb exploded on contact? He, Larner, and Cardis would be blown into eternity. Dineo shifted his gaze for a moment on Larner, whose right hand hung over the bomb release. The major's face had hardened and the veins of his fingers had almost burst through his flesh.

Then, when the plane came within twenty-five yards of the freighter, the major slammed the button with the palm of his hand. Simultaneously, with his other hand he shoved the stick forward and to his right. The Mitchell bomber leaped upwards and banked over the ship's rusting smokestack.

The copilot felt his muscles loosen. There was no explosion as the plane cleared the target. Not until the B-25 was 200 yards away did Dineo hear the concussion. Only then did he relax and grin.

"Right on the water line, Major; right on the water line."

"Pappy came up with another one," Larner returned the grin. "This'll make a difference. This'll sure as hell make a difference if they try to run another convoy to Lae."

Excited over this new experience, Joe Cardis also grinned as the B-25 curled away from the vessel. He had never whizzed at masthead height on a bombing run; only on strafing runs. It would seem odd indeed to see smoke and fire behind his attacking B-25 instead of reciprocal enemy fire. An eagerness gripped him, a desire to skip-bomb a real target.

As Ed Larner's plane circled over Merrick Bay, the next B-25 was veering away. Once more, the plane had moved more than 200 yards away from the ship, a respectable distance, before the explosion shook the sunken vessel. The delayed fuse had waited a patient five seconds, until the plane was safely away, before igniting the bomb.

The personnel watching from Port Moresby's shoreline felt an uneasiness. It seemed as though Merrick Bay was reliving the tragedy of a year ago; as though the B-25's were affronting the hallowed graves of men still entombed in the flooded compartments; as though the Mitchells were defacing sacred monuments.

When the four planes of Larner's lead flight had completed their runs, the fifth B-25 skimmed towards one of the sunken destroyers. Once more the pilot skillfully dropped his bombs and arched sharply skyward without mishap.

But then—tragedy. The sixth B-25 had failed to keep a safe distance behind the fifth plane. The pilot came in too soon and reached the target just as the skip bomb from the preceding plane exploded. Shrapnel and flying debris ripped off the wing of the B-25. The Mitchell cartwheeled over the sunken destroyer and splashed into the bay.

The pilot of the seventh plane slowed down instinctively after he loosened his fuse bomb. As he arched away, the fuse bomb exploded and metal fragments from the target tore into the plane's tail and fusilage. The plane jerked upwards and then fantailed towards the sea. However, the pilot managed to straighten out and bring the damaged plane to a crash landing on one of Port Moresby's airstrips.

"Goddam it! Goddam it!" Pappy Gunn cursed from the shoreline.

But General Whitehead was even more disturbed. He quickly radioed Major Larner: "Abort all aircraft; abort the practice mission." Then he called the Port Moresby naval station. "Request rescue craft at 1.4 in Merrick Bay. Out."

The launch had already been warmed up, simply waiting for the location. While the other B-25's circled away from the sunken ships, the navy launch skimmed quickly away from one of Port Moresby's jetties towards the stricken plane. But the battered Mitchell was sinking rapidly. Foaming water, curling around the plane's wings and fuselage like silver claws, yanked the B-25 to the bottom of Merrick Bay. By the time the launch had slid to a rocking halt at the crash site, only white eddies and two bobbing heads, those of the pilot and turret gunner, lay on the water's surface. The copilot was lost.

As soon as Whitehead had aborted the tests, Major Ed Larner and his crews returned to their Dobodura air base across the Owen Stanleys with their B-25's. Two hours later, Colonel Paul Gunn entered the 90th Squadron operations tent. Gunn had boarded the mail plane for the hundred-mile flight over the Owen Stanley Range and had quickly hurried to the squadron campsite. For a moment, Gunn stood motionless before the 90th Squadron pilots, his thick neck throbbing an angry red. Then he paced the floor irritably, his short, round body bouncing with every step. He flailed his arms, muttered under his breath, and rolled his cigar violently between his dense lips. Ed Larner sat at the edge of a desk with his head lowered. The other pilots in the operations tent followed the colonel's movements and gesticulations with a tinge of anxiety.

Finally, Gunn stopped, chomped on his cigar, and pointed the chewed Havana at the pilots standing around him. "I told you! I told you!" he screamed. "You were to stay fifteen seconds apart. Fifteen seconds! Those fuse bombs had meticulous timing devices. They wait eleven seconds from release and then—boom!" He shot both arms skyward.

"He simply miscalculated, Pappy," Larner said. "It could have happened to any of us."

"Anybody!" Pappy Gunn screamed again. "Why the hell do you think I came to the 3rd Group? I could've gotten any outfit in New Guinea to test those fuse bombs. You men are supposed to be the best, the most experienced pilots in the Southwest Pacific. Your group has been overseas for a year. Every one of you has flown at least twenty missions, including missions against Japanese shipping. You're supposed to be the best!" he emphasized with his pointed cigar. "But you foul up!" He sighed. "After what happened, the general might call the whole thing off."

Pappy Gunn soon had reason to voice his suspicions. However, it was not Whitehead who balked. Instead, it was General George Kenney, Fifth Air Force supreme commander in Brisbane, Australia.

NEWS OF THE TRAGEDY AND NEAR TRAGEDY at Merrick Bay reached the ears of Kenney at his Australian head-quarters. He immediately called General Whitehead in Port Moresby and demanded an explanation. When the deputy Fifth Air Force chief reported the circumstances sur-rounding the tests, General Kenney expressed dismay.

Destructive raids on Allied bases in New Guinea had badly depleted the already half-obsolete and understrengthed units of the Fifth Air Force. Worse, a high percentage of malaria-ridden airmen had been evacuated to the south for treatment, leaving a shortage of combat flight crews. In fact, the entire 22nd Bomb Group had been so understrengthed in aircraft, and its personnel so fatigued, that the entire group had been returned to Australia, pulled out of combat. Didn't General Whitehead himself realize that the 3rd Group itself had only three squadrons instead of four, and that even these three did not have a full complement of B-25's and A-20's? Didn't Whitehead also know that other air groups, like the 43rd Heavy Bomb Group, the Australian 9th Operational Group, and the 35th Fighter Group were equally under-strengthed in planes and combat crews?

Whitehead did know that Kenney's complaints were ac-curate. In fact, conditions were so bad, and the prospects of replacements so poor, that General Kenney could meet com-bat needs only by careful use of his planes and airmen. The Fifth Air Force commander had been working on a policy of rotation, wherein one-third of the aircraft would be kept in reserve, another one-third kept in maintenance in Australia, and only one-third of the aircraft on a combat-ready basis. The same was true of the combat crews.

In view of the shortages in men and aircraft, General Kenney grumbled irritably over the loss of only a single combat-ready plane, particularly in a noncombat accident. Kenney thus questioned Ennis Whitehead's judgment by en-dangering badly needed aircraft and airmen on this latest "Mad Professor" experiment.

However, General Whitehead hardly acknowledged Kenney's complaints. Instead, the Fifth Air Force ADVON commander in Port Moresby lashed back at his superior. He quickly reminded General Kenney that Colonel Pappy Gunn kept their aircraft intact with little more than spit and gum. Only through the remarkable efforts of the Mad Professor, in fact, could they keep as many planes as they did on a combat-ready basis. Whitehead also reminded the Fifth Air Force commander that it was Pappy Gunn's innovations that enabled Fifth Air Force to use the motley array of planes interchangeably: wing bombs on fighter planes to improvise these pursuit planes as bombers when no bombers were available; nose guns on B-25's and A-20's to use these planes as strafers and dive bombers when no fighters or dive bombers were available. It was unfair to criticize Pappy Gunn because of the tragedy at Merrick Bay.

General Kenney could do nothing but grudgingly agree with Whitehead's arguments. "Just tell them to be more careful," Kenney ended the conversation softly.

WHEN GENERAL WHITEHEAD RELAYED THE reprieve from General Kenney to Dobodura, Colonel Gunn, Major Larner, and the other 3rd Bomb Group airmen reacted gleefully. Despite the problems at Port Moresby, these airmen acknowledged the great potential of the skip bomb. The 90th Squadron airmen, now joined by the 89th Squadron airmen with their A-20's, enthusiastically joined Pappy Gunn in Oro Bay, where more sunken reminders of Japan's air superiority lay in the shallow harbor. For two days the B-25 and A-20 combat crews practiced their skip bombing techniques on a derelict destroyer, two rusting transports, and two corroding freighters. This time the 90th Squadron—and the 89th—suffered no damage. At the end of the second day, Major Larner announced to General Whitehead that the men of the 89th and 90th Squadrons, 3rd Bomb Group, were ready to use the skip bomb on live Japanese targets.

Twice during the month of February, 1943, reconnaissance planes reported ship convoys in the Solomon Sea between New Britain and eastern New Guinea. Larner and his pilots eagerly took off from their Dobodura base to meet the challenge with skip bombs. But, on both occasions, they failed to locate the reported Japanese convoys. Either the reports had been incorrect or the Japanese ship convoys had reached their destinations before the B-25's and A-20's could find them on the open sea.

"Don't fret," Pappy Gunn consoled the disappointed 3rd Bomb Group airmen. "The Japanese are not sitting idle in Rabaul. They've been fattening their air bases with more planes. So they'll sure as hell send more troops to New Guinea."

By late February, however, the excitement over the skip bomb had abated. The 3rd Group airmen merely practiced now and then to keep sharp. 90th and 89th Squadron crews, along with other Fifth Air Force units, reverted to the routine of attacking the Japanese bases of Lae, Madang, and Wewak along New Guinea's northern coast. Sometimes the American airmen returned with good results and sometimes they came back with poor results—normal for the New Guinea air campaign.

Then, during the last week in February, 1943, General Ennis Whitehead received an intelligence report from Aussie jungle watchers in New Britain:

> Something big in the wind at Rabaul. Simpson
> Harbor jammed with ships. Japanese bigwigs
> coming to Rabaul. Will report any new develop-
> ments.

The unidentified bigwigs referred to in the coded message were General Hatazo Adachi, commander of the Japanese Eighteenth Army in New Guinea; Admiral Masatomi Kimura, of the Japanese Eighth Fleet; Vice Admiral Gunichi Mikawa, supreme commander of the Eighth Fleet in the Southwest Pacific area; General Rimpei Ota, commander of the 7th Air Division in New Guinea; General Sato Nakano, commander of the elite 51st Japanese Infantry Division, and Admiral Jinichi Kusaka, commander of the Eleventh Air Fleet in Rabaul.

General Whitehead frowned when he read the intelligence message from New Britain. "I wonder what the hell they're up to?" he said to Pappy Gunn.

Nobody in New Guinea knew what the Japanese were up to, but the two American air corps officers would soon understand the crucial significance of the skip bomb.

Chapter Three

KIMURA'S CONVOY

Rabaul: The Japanese stronghold at New Britain in the Southwest Pacific. The Japanese bastion was the most heavily defended point in the Bismarck Archipelago, for the base was the heart of Japan's Southwest Pacific war. From this New Britain fortress Japan fed men and supplies to her bases in New Guinea, Bougainville, Cape Gloucester, and the Solomons to maintain her superiority over the Allies. From here lurked the submarines and destroyers and cruisers that preyed on Allied ships plying through the Solomon and Bismarck Seas. From here the flocks of Betty bombers and Zero fighters lashed out at the string of Allied airfields and supply depots in New Guinea and the Solomons.

Rabaul was the counterpart of the Allies' Port Moresby, 475 air miles away. The base offered two harbors capable of sheltering fleets—Blanche Bay and Simpson Harbor. Rabaul commanded the approaches to Australia and the South Pacific, and the Japanese had seized Rabaul hungrily in early 1942 during their thrust to the South Pacific. Quickly, they had built a major supply, naval, air, army, and staging base in the bowl-shaped flats of kunai plains. A horseshoe range of mountains behind the base and harbors made impossible any attempt to wrest the base by ground action. And so, the Japanese operated smugly and confidently from inside Rabaul's bowl.

Rabaul was vital for any Allied plan to thrust northward from New Guinea.

Thus, as Operation 157 necessitated the capture or reduction of Port Moresby, so too General Douglas MacArthur's visions of a reconquest with Operation Elkton depended on the capture or reduction of Rabaul.

At Rabaul, the common Japanese soldier, like his American GI counterpart, registers a sense of awe when he sees an assemblage of high brass, for such conferences undoubtedly affect him. Japanese service troops going about their busy routines in Rabaul stopped in their work to watch vehicles carrying the flags of admirals and generals as the vehicles headed for the winding, uphill dirt road that led to General Hitoshi Imamura's bungalow. Non-com superiors, just as awed, did not scold the curious soldiers.

Those closest to the hillside quarters of Imamura could clearly see the general standing stiffly on the porch steps of his bungalow, where two other high-ranking officers stood erectly on either side of him. An array of medals shone from Imamura's gray uniform. The sheaf of his sword sparkled in the tropic sun, and the hem of his coat fluttered in the soft breeze.

On the approach of two visitors striding briskly towards the bungalow, General Imamura stepped off the porch and extended his right hand in greeting. The two visitors, one a general and the other an admiral, bowed respectfully before Imamura, and then reached out to grasp the extended hand.

"Honorable commander," General Adachi said, "may the gods reward you for giving us this audience."

Imamura nodded and then, when he shifted his gaze on the other visitor, the admiral, an aura of respect beamed from the general's eyes. The second visitor was the highly esteemed Eel of the Pacific, Vice Admiral Masatomi Kimura.

"I too thank the honorable commander," Admiral Kimura told General Imamura. The admiral then looked at the two officers standing one step up behind Imamura. Kimura nodded a greeting to Admiral Gunichi Mikawa, commander of the Imperial Eighth Fleet and to Admiral Jinichi Kasaka, commander of the Imperial Eleventh Air Fleet. The two superiors acknowledged Kimura with a nod.

"Come, come inside," General Imamura said. "The general staff awaits us."

When the five high-ranking officers disappeared into the bungalow, non-com superiors hustled their toiling service troops back to work. The show was over.

One of the paradoxes of the Pacific war was the chain of authority among military commanders.

The United States, a free and democratic nation, left full authority in the hands of supreme commanders. The President, for instance, could make any decision he chose, ignoring the suggestions of his counsel. So too could General Douglas MacArthur or Admiral Chester Nimitz, the navy commander in the Pacific. Although American leaders did enlist advisors, none was bound by them and they could ignore any suggestions with an autocratic decision that brought no criticism or repercussion. More often than not, in fact, most war strategy was based on the sole decision of an American commander.

Conversely, Imperial Japan was supposed to be a totalitarian state where all subjects bowed without question to the Emperor or his designated authority. Yet, military commanders never made individual decisions. They always elicited suggestions and recommendations from subordinates in a conference room, and some staff decisions could even go against the wishes of the Emperor. Therefore, all military decisions were hammered out from a multitude of different ideas. Operation 157, although announced as a command order from General Imamura, was really the decision of the Eighth Area Imperial Japanese Staff.

Now, in this last week of February, the Japanese general staff of the Eighth Area Headquarters assembled in the conference room of General Hitoshi Imamura's bungalow. Besides the foursome on the porch who had joined Imamura, at least a dozen other officers, from army colonels to navy captains on up, had joined Imamura. The array of Japanese military brass soon gathered around a large table on which aides had spread a huge map of the Bismarck Archipelago: The islands of New Britain and New Guinea, the Solomon Sea, the Bismarck Sea, Guadalcanal, and all other islands, gulfs, channels, and straits in between the points on the map.

WHEN GENERAL IMAMURA OPENED THE conference, he nodded to General Adachi. The Eighteenth Army commander did not hesitate. He placed the tip of a forefinger on the huge map: Wau.

"Here is the cancer that must be destroyed if Operation 157 is to culminate in a reconquest of New Guinea." He straightened, looked about the general staff and raised a single finger. "One division is all we shall need; one fresh, trustworthy division of troops, fully equipped with guns and supplies. Such a reinforcement will enable us to successfully launch Operation 157."

The staff of army, air force, and naval officers standing about the table said nothing. They already knew that Adachi had come to plead for New Guinea reinforcements. They knew also of Adachi's obsession against the Australian base of Wau, high in the Owen Stanley Range. Rather, the staff was concerned with the consequences of Adachi's request.

Would such reinforcements truly enable Japan to oust the Allies from New Guinea? The Tokyo Express had already sent hundreds of fresh troops into Guadalcanal against the American marines. However, the Americans held the island more firmly now than at any time since the initial marine landings in August of 1942. Further, Adachi's request would require a huge convoy. Could the Japanese navy carry such a convoy safely to Lae, and could the air force protect the convoy against air attacks?

The staff officers fell into small groups to discuss the merits of reinforcing New Guinea on this large scale. Some argued that a large convoy might suffer heavy damage when it entered Huon Gulf and came into range of light and medium Allied bombers. And, based on past experience in the Solomons, they doubted that such reinforcements would change the stalemate in New Guinea.

Other staff members argued that they had already approved Operation 157, a plan that called for troop reinforcements to New Guinea. They also believed that failure in the Solomons came about because they had brought troops there piecemeal instead of sending one huge force of ground troops at once to overwhelm the enemy. Further, the convoy that had carried the 102nd Brigade to Lae in January had been attacked, but the Allied Fifth Air Force had been too feeble to inflict any serious damage.

The conferees now sought the opinions of Kusaka, Mikawa, and General Nakano. Admiral Kusaka, commander of the Eleventh Air Fleet, expressed optimism. The air arm in the Bismarck Archipelago was actually directed by the Imperial Navy, including Eleventh Air Fleet units in New Britain and New Guinea. Its commander, Admiral Jinichi Kusaka, had been a successful carrier pilot.

Admiral Kusaka acknowledged that the Japanese air divisions in the Bismarck Archipelago far exceeded in number of planes the estimated number of Fifth Air Force planes. The Eleventh Air Fleet had over 200 planes on their New Guinea bases alone, and they could call on several hundred more planes from other Japanese bases, including Rabaul.

Admiral Gunichi Mikawa, commander of the Eighth Fleet, said their surface navy in the Southern Pacific area was strong and healthy. The fleet included several cruisers, two dozen destroyers, and numerous freighters and troop transports. They could even enlist two battleships from Truk, the Central Pacific base, if necessary. Further, Admiral Mineichi Koga, commander of the combined Japanese Pacific fleets in Truk, had assured Admiral Mikawa that the Eighth Fleet commander could have more naval vessels if he wanted them. Therefore, Admiral Kimura could have all the surface ships he wanted to carry a convoy to Lae.

General Sato Nakano of the 51st Division said his men were primed, ready, and eager to make the voyage to New Guinea for a new fight against the Allies.

Thus, the eyes of the staff now fell on Admiral Masatomi Kimura, the designated commander for the proposed Lae Resupply Convoy. The slim, sober-faced admiral was a quiet man who weighed his words carefully before he spoke. His sharp piercing eyes carried the weight of authority and determination. And, on the basis of his past record, others listened when he spoke.

Kimura had been on the Imperial Japanese naval staff in both Tokyo and on Truk Island before he actively joined the Outer Sea Fleets for combat duty. During the Solomons campaign, Admiral Kimura had been more successful than any other fleet commander on the Tokyo Express down the Slot from Rabaul to Guadalcanal. The soft-spoken admiral had made several runs through the Slot and he had suffered the loss of only one transport and damage to two destroyers. His daring and his cunning had earned him the respected title: Eel of the Pacific. Kimura thus enjoyed great esteem among the Japanese general staff and total loyalty from the sailors under his command.

Some had wondered why Kimura had not risen in rank, although rumor said his frequent disagreements with top naval brass had delayed promotion. On this point, he acted much like General Ennis Whitehead. But here, all similarities ended between the calm, deliberate Kimura and the rasping, impatient Whitehead.

Kimura had consulted with General Adachi before this staff meeting and the Eighteenth Army commander had convinced the Eel of the Pacific that large reinforcements could break the stalemate in New Guinea. So, Kimura had already made tentative plans to direct a large convoy from Rabaul to Lae. He was now prepared to place this plan before the Eighth Area staff.

"I believe we can make this voyage to Lae without undue difficulty," Kimura began in his soft, deliberate voice. "My own staff has worked out a careful strategy for such a voyage. And surely, if, as the honorable Adachi believes, such reinforcements will wrest the initiative from our enemies, then we should give General Adachi's suggestion our most serious consideration. I, personally, strongly favor the proposed Lae Resupply Convoy."

The positive statements from Kusaka, Mikawa, Nakano, and now Kimura impressed the staff. It was now left to General Adachi to win a final approval from the general staff.

Adachi spoke in the same familiar terms. The Allies were too weak to repel a new offensive. The Fifth Air Force was badly depleted, unable to do anything more than deliver minor stings against Japan's New Guinea bases and ship convoys. The American navy had not yet recovered from the Japanese naval punches in the Solomons. Adachi even quoted Admiral Nimitz, commander of the American Pacific naval forces: "It now appears that we are unable to control the seas in the Southwest Pacific areas." Finally, Adachi reminded the staff that the three Allied combat divisions in eastern New Guinea had been left disease ridden and understrengthed from the Buna campaign. They would be no match for fresh troops.

And, according to Japanese intelligence, Washington had ignored the Allied call for reinforcements in the Southwest Pacific, preferring instead to use their resources in the European theater of war.

"What better hour can we find than this hour to strike against our enemies?" Adachi concluded.

The Eighteenth Army commander had successfully delivered the clincher and the Eighth Area general staff approved the proposed Lae Resupply Convoy. When the decision was reached, General Hitoshi Imamura shuttled his dark eyes between General Adachi and Admiral Kimura. A tint of satisfaction was reflected on his face.

"For many weeks have I meditated on a new offensive against the Americans and Australians. How I implored help from my honorable ancestors and how I prayed in thanks when the 102nd Brigade landed safely in Lae. Now, Adachi-*san*, my heart is lightened by your confidence and enthusiasm. You shall have more than the well-trained 51st Combat Division; the elite 77th Imperial Brigade will also be at your disposal."

Imamura then turned to Admiral Kimura. "And to you, Kimura-*san*, may the samurai spirits be your guide on this voyage to Lae. I feel in my heart that the gods are with us."

Admiral Gunichi Mikawa also turned to Masatomi Kimura to wish him luck. He offered Kimura two cruisers and eight destroyers with which to escort six troop transports, four freighters, and two oil tankers into Lae.

When Kimura nodded, General Imamura looked about the general staff. "A toast to the success of our mission. Let us pray that within the year we can offer another toast from a new headquarters in Australia."

THE SUN BURST IN A HUGE LAVENDER ball on the morning of February 26, 1943. Its rays slanted through the emerging day like purple tentacles. They reached out across the sky to touch the horseshoe-shaped Rabaul Range that cupped the huge base and its twin harbors in a protective semi-circle.

Within the range's bowl, the flood of early sunlight had covered with a hue of pink the array of small buildings in

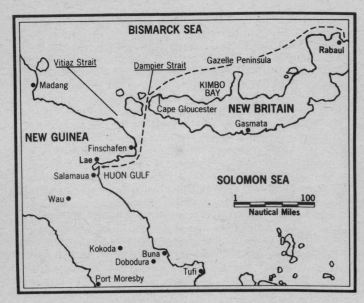

Map 2: Proposed route of Admiral Kimura's Lae Resupply Convoy.

Rabaul township. And they had settled a film of silver on the laden docks and jetties along the shore of Simpson Harbor. Finally, the emerging daylight had exposed the bustling activity in and around the oblong lagoon of Simpson Harbor. Service personnel were shaping the Lae Resupply Convoy.

From the seven wharves protruding out of the Vulcan Crater Peninsula, which separated Simpson Harbor from Blanche Bay, barges plied heavily through the nestled waters. Their drafts bulged with battle-clad Japanese soldiers. As the boats puttered towards waiting *maru* transports, the troops laughed or prattled playfully. They sang songs of Fujiyama, cherry blossom time, geisha houses, or the tea houses of Tokyo.

Those still waiting on shore stirred about in jocular restlessness. Some jerked the green belts that held their ammo packs and medical kits. Others tilted their glossy tan helmets to better peer into the bay. A few straightened the wrap-around leggings that covered the calves of their legs.

The morale of the 77th Imperial Brigade and the 51st Infantry Division was quite high.

And while the fully uniformed troops shuttled to the anchored transports in Simpson Harbor, spectators congregated on the shoreline in ever-increasing numbers. They represented the curious, the hopeful, or the disappointed; sons of Japan who would not make the trip to New Guinea to avenge the loss of the Solomons, Kokoda, and Buna.

But the movement of troops was only a part of the activity in the calm lagoon. Long hoses, ten inches in diameter, ran across a series of pontoons from the oil storage depots in the still-silhouetted trees on Simpson Harbor's northern shore. Since midnight the monotonous clackity-clack of generators had accompanied the pumping of fuel into the two tankers lying offshore—fuel oil, aviation gas, truck gas, lubricating oil. Hour after hour, the tankers dropped deeper and deeper into the bay. When the level scale on the hulls registered a fourteen-foot draft, the tankers would be fully loaded.

Nor was there idleness around Blanche Bay on the eastern side of the Vulcan Crater protrusion. The Lukani Peninsula on the north shore of the bay was a flat, two-square-mile area of jungle that served as the main material center of the Japanese base. Here, deep in concrete storage areas, the Japanese 8th Supply Depot maintained a six-month inventory of supplies—from bandages to thousand-pound bombs, from *sake* to rice, from small wire to huge generators. The peninsula's thick foliage also hid from the snooping lenses of reconnaissance planes Rabaul's repair facilities and the harborage for small boats and barges.

The rising sun awoke the Lukani Peninsula as it had awakened Simpson Harbor. From the Lukani service area, endless streams of motor launches weaved past the anchored warships in Blanche Bay. They hooked around the Vulcan Crater Peninsula's Matupi Point and skimmed into the sheltered Simpson Harbor. They carried ammo, food, guns, medicine, and other materials to the four anchored *maru* freighters. Some carried tanks, artillery, or trucks. Huge floating cranes, with the aid of stevedores, scooped tons of equipment and supplies and hoisted them onto the cargo decks where sharp-eyes superiors directed operations. Deck hands lowered and stashed the array of crates into the holds, then chained big guns and vehicles onto the decks. Not until they had filled the huge bellies and jammed the wide decks of the 7,000-ton freighters would activity stop.

General Imamura had just finished breakfast and stepped out onto the porch of his neat, white bungalow. His residence, on a knoll snuggled against the Rabaul Range, overlooked the township, the airstrips west and south of the town, the docks and jetties of Simpson Harbor and Blanche Bay. For some moments he watched the anthill efforts in and around Simpson Harbor. Then he squinted at the misty gray outlines of Kimura's warships lying in Blanche Bay. A satisfied smile creased his face.

"Does all go well, Imamura-*san?*" General Adachi was suddenly standing next to him. The Eighteenth Army commander, a guest in Imamura's bungalow, had followed his superior to the porch and was also scanning the activities around Rabaul.

"In two days the armada will sail," Imamura said. "Admiral Kusaka assures me that the Eleventh Air Fleet will have 300 interceptors ready for escort. And in New Guinea, the 7th Air Division will prepare another 200 aircraft for possible escort duty on this voyage to Lae."

"What of Admiral Kimura?"

"The esteemed Kimura will honor us with lunch," Adachi said. "Now, he meets with his staff aboard his flagship. Will you sail with him?"

"No. I and my staff will sail to Lae aboard the destroyer *Tokitsukaze,*" Adachi said. "General Nakano and his 51st Division staff will sail aboard the *Yukikaze.*"

Imamura nodded.

"The troops of our Eighteenth Army will burst with joy when they learn we bring fresh troops to join them. I will speak to the Admiral at lunch," Adachi finished.

AT THAT MOMENT, ADMIRAL MASATOMI KIMURA was not thinking of lunch. In the chart room of the cruiser *Shirayuki,* he had gathered his staff and ship commanders: troop transport commander Captain Kametaro Matsumoto, cargo ship commander Captain Mirioru Genda, Security chief Captain Yusi Watanabe, and Kimura's own executive officer, Captain Yukata Tishayuna.

Kimura had spread a large map on a polished desk of teakwood. The admiral wore his dark, formal naval coat and the array of colorful battle ribbons as well as the Eighth Fleet insignia sparkling on his left chest. Further, he stood hatless in contrast to the several officers around him, who wore their whites. They mumbled to each other in low, informal tones as they waited for Kimura to speak. After the staff decision, Admiral Kimura would be in complete charge and his word would be absolute law on the voyage to Lae.

When Kimura tapped the map with the point of a thick samurai cane, the idle chatter stopped. The staff members planted their feet in comfortable stances on the red-carpeted deck and looked at the sober-faced commander, watching his dark, penetrating eyes.

"Gentlemen," Kimura began, "the Americans are not fools. Although our interceptor forces are strong, our warning system unsurpassed, some American reconnaissance aircraft will no doubt observe the activity begun today in Rabaul. But the enemy can only speculate. If we remain cautious, alert, and mobile, the Americans will learn nothing of our mission or route to Lae. Thus, our plans must be certain and well understood."

Kimura now turned the meeting over to his executive officer, Captain Yukata Tishayuna, who would brief the ship captains on the route, time, speed, and other particulars of their mission.

The convoy of 22 ships would leave Rabaul at 2300 hours, an hour before midnight on the evening of February 28, and they would arrive in Lae sometime on March 3. The convoy would sail out of Rabaul's Simpson Harbor and Blanche Bay, circle around the Rabaul Peninsula, and then head directly west into the Bismarck Sea. They would sail through the open sea and then hug the coast of the Gazelle Peninsula through the night. By dawn of March 1, they would reach Kimbo Bay and would then hug the coastline of New Britain until dusk, when they would again sail into the open waters through the night. On the third period of daylight they would cut through the Dampier Strait between New Britain and Rooke Island.

Up to the Dampier Strait, the convoy could expect little problem with American bombers, since only long-range, heavy bombers could reach this far from Dobodura or Port Moresby, and efficient helmsmen could easily avoid high-level attacks. But once beyond the Dampier Strait into the

Solomon Sea, they would be in range of medium and light bombers. So for most of the third day they would be sailing exposed through the Solomon Sea and Huon Gulf.

"But," Captain Tishayuna pointed out, "General Kusaka has assured us that not for a minute will we be without air cover. Our aircraft will hover above us like a protective umbrella all the way from the Dampier Strait to Lae. At least one squadron from the 7th Air Division in Lae, Wewak, or Madang will always be with us; and we can call on more aircraft if needed. The pitiful U.S. Fifth Air Force will be no problem for us."

As for American submarines, the Japanese anticipated little problem here. American subs had thus far done poorly in the Southwest Pacific, mostly because the subs were old, badly in need of maintenance, and their torpedo crews were hastily trained. Further, American subs were based in Australia, too far to be an effective weapon against the convoy.

And, as usual, Tishayuna continued, the convoy would maintain the *hochi* pattern, keeping a thousand yards distant from each other with a cruiser and three destroyers protecting the flank. A seventh destroyer would patrol the van, and an eighth destroyer would patrol the rear.

"Is all understood?" Kimura now spoke.

His subordinates nodded.

"Then let us show courage and determination," Admiral Kimura said. "The voyage may have elements of danger, but if each man calmly does his part, we will succeed in bringing this giant striking force to Lae. I will drink with you a toast, gentlemen; then I must dine with General Imamura and the honorable Adachi before we sail."

BY EARLY EVENING OF FEBRUARY 28, 1943, the bristling activity in Rabaul had ended. The weary service troops of the 8th Supply Depot were resting after three days of hectic toil. The curious, the hopeful, and the disappointed had deserted the docks and jetties around Simpson Harbor.

The twelve thousand troops of the 51st Division were settled aboard the smaller 6,000-ton *maru* transports. The more elite 77th Brigade occupied the two larger transports, the 10,000-ton *Nojima Maru* and the 8,000-ton *Kyoikusei Maru*. The two tankers and four freighters, loaded to the last

SPOOK

Colonel Paul "Pappy" Gunn *(below, right)* devised skip bomb technique, and Major Ed Larner *(above)* led attack on convoy.

Pictured is Col. Bob Strickland, commander 3rd Bomb Group, whose aircraft finished off Lae Resupply Convoy. Below, ordnance crews haul skip bombs to waiting B-25's.

FIFTH AIR FORCE

5th Air Force brass: Top left is Gen. Ennis Whitehead, who directed Operation Bismarck Sea from Port Moresby; top right is Gen. George Kenney, Commanding General, 5th Air Force; at left is organizational emblem.

Official U.S. Air Force Photo

Crew of "Torrid Tessie, the Terror" pose with their plane. It is a B-25, capable of low-level bombings. Note heavy camouflage.

Official U.S. Air Force Photo

On an inspection tour, Lt. Gen. William Knudsen is met by Generals Whitehead *(center)* and Kenney. Standing by "Yellow Fever" are Lt. Ed Richardson of Muskogee, Okla., S/Sgt. Herb Marion of Ryderwood, Wash., T/Sgt. Lawrence Pack of Jefferson, Ore., Sgt. George Moon of Longview, Texas.

Official U.S. Air Force Photo

Official U.S. Air Force Photo

A 1943 meeting at Port Moresby involving, left to right, Col. Prentis, Lt. Gen. Kenney, Maj. Gen. Sutherland, Gen. MacArthur.

Official U.S. Air Force Photo

Official U.S. Air Force Photo

2nd Lt. Kenneth C. Sparks of Blackwell, Okla., left, and Capt. Thomas J. Lynch of Catasauqua, Pa., each brought his total of air victories to nine during the Battle of the Bismarck Sea.

Official U.S. Air Force Photo

Aerial view of strip at Port Moresby, showing revetments for B-17 "Flying Fortress" planes on the dispersal area.

available square foot, lay like half-sunken ships, their gunwhales only a dozen feet out of the water. On the decks of the freighters, all available space was occupied by trucks, tanks, and guns.

In Blanche Bay, the warships, quiet and still, were becoming silhouettes in the growing darkness. Japanese sailors leaned against the railings of the eight destroyers and two cruisers, looking into the depths of Simpson Harbor and the town beyond, wondering if they might once more meet with friends and comrades who occupied Rabaul. A sense of nostalgia competed with a sense of eagerness, for Kimura's sailors, too, saw in this great armada the road to a lost glory.

Many of these sailors were veterans of the naval death struggles in the Ironbottom Strait during the Guadalcanal campaign. The destroyer *Uranami* had fought in several engagements, including the Battle of Guadalcanal where she fearlessly exchanged fire with the battleship *South Dakota*. The destroyer *Asagumo* had distinguished itself in the same battle, pelting several American destroyers and almost breaking up the fight before it started. *Asagumo* had also suffered scars in the Battle of Cape Esperance. The destroyer *Arishio* had served in several Solomon Island fights and had rescued Admiral Nagumo in the Battle of Cape Esperance. The destroyer *Hatsuyuki* and her crew had been part of the three-destroyer team that finished off the destroyers *Little* and *Gregory* and damaged the cruisers *Boise* and *San Francisco* at Cape Esperance. She was the only ship to come out of the battle unscathed. Destroyers *Shikanami* and *Yukikaze* had fearlessly plied into the American battle wagons during the Battle of Guadalcanal, trading their five-inch shells for fourteen-inch shells.

The cruiser *Tenryu* had been one of the big killers in the Battle of Savo Island where Japanese sailors sank several Allied warships. Twice *Tenryu* had been reported sunk, but she was still alive and her crews ready to fight again. Finally, the *Shirayuki*, Kimura's flagship, had been the highest scorer in the Battle of Cape Esperance, rolling up hundreds of hits on American naval vessels while she found time to rescue hundreds of Japanese sailors during the fight.

So, Adachi could not have asked for anything better than these battle-scarred warships and veteran sailors to escort his reinforcements into Lae.

By late evening, the tropic air had cooled over Rabaul. A soft, southeasterly breeze rocked slightly the tops of trees surrounding Simpson Harbor and sent small ripples across the lagoon. The big Rabaul complex was almost totally dark. Most of the garrison had retired for the night, taking advantage of the cooling breezes and low humidity, a rarity in the Southwest Pacific jungles.

Suddenly a blinking signal light pierced the darkness of Blanche Bay. The convoy's flagship, *Shirayuki*, was signaling the *Arishio*, the flagship of the destroyer division. In turn, *Arishio* signaled other ships. Soon, the lights had leapfrogged into Simpson Harbor, where the merchant ships were soon engaged in incandescent conversations. For several moments the blinkers flashed back and forth across Simpson Harbor and Blanche Bay, as though the harbors had come alive with fireflies. But then, one by one, the lights winked out.

Finally, at 2300, the last blinker, aboard the *Shirayuki*, went dark.

A spurt of heavy smoke curled out of the *Shirayuki*'s twin smokestacks and rose upwards in a black coil against the darkened sky. Slowly the sleek cruiser glided out of the bay. Other ships soon trailed in its wake.

Twenty-two ships soon rendezvoused into a *hochi* pattern in St. George's Channel. Six transports with 15,000 troops crisscrossed into columns of twos. Behind them came the two tankers with 30,000 gallons of oil in their holds. Finally, in a diamond pattern, came the four heavily laden freighters puffing black smoke. On either side of the merchant ships were three of the destroyers and one cruiser. To the rear, a destroyer moved back and forth as a trailing picket. The last destroyer, the *Asashio*, sliced forward of the convoy. She then moved in a steady zig-zag at 16 knots, acting as the vanguard picket for the convoy.

By midnight the 22 ships, the largest Japanese convoy assembled since the invasion of the Philippines more than a year ago, steamed into the open Bismarck Sea. By morning the Lae Resupply Convoy would be halfway to the Gazelle Peninsula—and several hours closer to General Hatazo Adachi's dreams of reconquest.

Chapter Four

CONVOY IN SIGHT!

Every Allied soldier, airman, and sailor in the Southwest Pacific worried about Rabaul. They could trace most Japanese sea raids and air raids to Rabaul. They knew that most Japanese ground reinforcements to the Solomons and New Guinea came from Rabaul. They also heard it was heavily fortified, practically impenetrable. So strong was this base, in fact, that General Douglas MacArthur would bypass it on his return to the Philippines in the fall of 1944.

However, not only Rabaul offered a deterrent to Operation Elkton, MacArthur's plan to recapture the Philippines. Just across the Bismarck Sea from New Britain, west-northwest, lay the Admiralties, a pair of islands under Japanese occupation since January of 1942. If, under the Elkton Plan, MacArthur could bypass New Britain on the way to the Philippines, he could not bypass the Admiralties. The islands sat in the center of the thousand-mile-square Bismarck Archipelago that made up the battle area of the Southwest Pacific. The Admiralties, in fact, lay directly athwart the New Guinea-Philippine axis. Thus, the islands posed a threat to any potential movement westward across the Pacific from the Caroline Islands chain or any movement up the New Guinea coast. Any attempt at a counteroffensive against Japan in the Western Pacific necessitated the capture of the Admiralties.

The Admiralties, encompassing the islands of Manus and Los Negros, were first discovered by Dutch sailors in the early 17th century. However, the Dutch did not explore these islands until a century later when an adventurous captain, Phillip Carteret, made forays through the islands in the 1760s. But even he found the islands too humid for comfort and the Dutch continued to ignore their find. However, in 1880 the more ambitious Germans occupied the islands and opened rubber and coconut plantations. In 1920, after World War I, defeated Germany ceded the islands to England, who renamed the islands the Admiralties in honor of their navy. The British, in turn, mandated the islands to their Southwest Pacific commonwealth, Australia.

The Australians, however, did little here because of the dense humidity, oppressive heat, and heavy rainfall. Less than fifty Australians governed the more than 12,000 natives. So these natives continued their primitive ways with little interruption from the Australians.

Thus, when Japanese troops landed on Los Negros and Manus in early 1942, they met no Allied opposition. At first, the Japanese had not seen any value in these islands except as part of the overall occupation of the East Indies. Not until mid-1942 did Japan recognize the Admiralties' strategic location in the Bismarck Archipelago, which by now had become the center of the Japanese-Allied struggle in the Southwest Pacific.

Japanese military leaders soon built two airstrips, the Momote Drome on Los Negros and the Lorengeau Airdrome on the larger island of Manus. Further, they developed Seedler Bay into a major harbor where they could shelter and service naval task forces. Until 1943, the Admiralties were too far away from Papua for most air strikes. Only a few available heavy bombers occasionally struck the Admiralties with poor to moderate results. So the Japanese worked fervently to strengthen the Admiralties.

In February of 1943 Allied reconnaissance planes noted something new in the islands. The Japanese were building an oil refinery and they already built several huge oil storage tanks. Imperial Japanese headquarters had apparently decided to refine their confiscated East Indies oil in the battle zones instead of shipping the crude oil back to Japan for refinement and reshipment to the Southwest Pacific war zone. The savings in time, money, and potential ship losses would greatly strengthen their operations in the Southwest Pacific area.

On February 27, 1943, Allied reconnaissance photos showed that oil storage tanks had been completed on both Manus and Los Negros. Also, an oil refinery on Manus Island was almost completed. When General Ennis Whitehead saw the report, he scowled at an aide. "That's all we need: a Japanese refinery a step away from their combat forces. Send out the 3rd and 38th. They can hit the place at low level."

The aide nodded.

ON THE LATE MORNING OF MARCH 1, 1943, ninety airmen of the 3rd Bomb Group, including several photographers, jammed themselves into the air unit's operation tent. The scorching sun was already penetrating the canvas. There was no breeze and the stifling humidity radiated through the interior of the three-poled tent. The briefing, only a few minutes old, had already left the battle-clad flyers restless and uncomfortable. Sweat dampened their faces and perspiration itched their bodies under the heavy, fur-lined jackets. Standing before them was the group commander, Colonel Bob Strickland, a hardened, veteran bomber pilot.

Strickland had been in the Southwest Pacific over a year, flying B-25's against overwhelming odds in the early battle against the Japanese. He had been part of that 1942 island hopping group who flew into Mindanao to bomb Japanese airfields so the 19th Bomb Group could escape from Delmonte and return most of their B-17's to Australia. He had also been involved in the air strikes at Kokoda in the Owen Stanleys that had stopped the Japanese advance towards Port Moresby. Perhaps he should have been rotated home to the states by now, but Strickland was too experienced, too capable, and too well respected by the men of the 3rd Group. Fifth Air Force did not want to lose such a man.

"This attack on the Admiralties will be our most ambitious raid," Colonel Strickland said. He pointed to a huge map behind him. "Recon is certain: there's a huge refinery under construction right here east of Momote Drome on the Admiralties' Los Negros Island. The Japs have also built storage tanks just south of Momote Drome—here, along the west shore of Porha Lake, and here—on Manus Island." He moved a finger along the wall map behind him. "They've got more storage tanks near Lorengeau Airdrome."

"Why us, Colonel?" one of the officers asked.

"Because heavies may miss from high altitude. Anyway, we don't have enough B-17's and B-24's to do the job. They've already done one hell of a job on the airstrips, hangars, and repair facilities. But the Japs are keeping their storage tanks well hidden. We and the 38th can come in low, under a hundred feet, and be certain of hitting them."

Colonel Strickland turned back to the map and continued the briefing. The Mitchells would fly in seven diamond patterns all the way to target, some 700 miles distant. The B-25's of the 38th Group would strike at the oil storage tanks near Lorengeau Airdome on Manus Island and the 3rd Group would hit Los Negros, with the B-25's hitting the tanks at Porha Lake and the A-20 flights hitting the refinery. The aircraft would carry either 500- or 250-pound bombs, with some of the medium bombers carrying 30-pound clusters for more precise bombing. Finally, three of the A-20's would come in with napalm bombs to finish the job.

"What about escort?" somebody asked.

Strickland told the airmen that P-38's from both the 49th and 35th Fighter Groups, about 35 planes, would provide air cover. Further, both fighter planes and bombers would carry auxiliary gasoline wing tanks because the flight would detour south of Rooke Island instead of flying past Cape Gloucester in New Britain. Such a detour would entail a 750-mile, one-way flight instead of the direct 600-mile flight. Thus, they would need auxiliary gas tanks.

However, the detoured flight path would avoid Japanese spotters who could warn the Japanese in the Admiralties that American bombers were coming across the Bismarck Sea for an apparent strike at Los Negros, Manus, or both. Further, swarms of fighter planes from Cape Gloucester, Madang, Wewak, or Lae could easily throw plenty of heat at the 40 bombers and 35 P-38's as the planes droned over the Bismarck Sea. Acutely aware of this, Strickland had charted a course that minimized the opportunity of detection. Further, the aircraft would approach the Admiralties at sea level to avoid radar and, hopefully, hit the target with a surprise assault.

Strickland estimated their arrival at target at about 1300 hours. He also established a 144.5 east by .05 south location as the area of rendezvous after the raid. The 3rd and 38th Groups would then return to their Dobodura base by the same detour. Strickland warned his pilots they could expect heavy interceptor attacks after they left the target because the Japanese would then know that B-25's and A-20's had been to the Admiralties.

But there was a bright spot. Weather forecasters had predicted a heavy weather front over the Bismarck Archipelago sometime this afternoon. The front would enable the bombers to lose potential interceptors in the thick clouds. In fact, the mission had been scheduled later in the day for that very reason—to take advantage of the predicted weather front.

"If you have to ditch," Strickland continued, "radio the Aussies. They have our flight plan and they'll send out PBY searchers if any of you are down. That's why it's important you stay in the planned flight path. And, of course, if ack-ack or Zekes cripple you, try to get to Wau. They'll have emergency crews waiting for you."

At 1100 hours the morning of March 1, 1943, the sixteen B-25's and twelve A-20's of the 3rd Bomb Group taxied onto Dobodura's main runway and took off for the long flight through the Japanese-held segment of the Bismarck Archipelago. Right behind them came the twelve B-25's of the 38th Bomb Group. Although the entire flight would be over water, few of the airmen believed they could fly the 750 miles without detection. Pilots and copilots checked and rechecked their instruments. Gunners checked and rechecked their 50-caliber guns.

And, as the bombers, headed for the open sea, the airmen stayed alert. They did not relish the long flight northwestward to the Bismarck Sea. But whatever their thoughts, none of them could guess that a heavily laden, 22-ship Japanese convoy was also heading west into the

Bismarck Sea and the red pages of military history.

AS THE TWENTY-EIGHT B-25'S AND TWELVE A-20's
approached the Vitiaz Strait, over 200 miles from Dobodura,
misty specks in the distance caught the eyes of turret gunners. When the specks grew larger, the gunners could see the
twin fuselages—P-38's. The gunners relaxed and even felt a
sense of security as the Lightning fighters pulled alongside
the bombers and hung next to them like suspended spiders.

A few of the P-38's scooted far ahead of the bomber formations, dipping, diving, disappearing, and reappearing like
restless fledglings testing their wings. These Lightnings
were searching for possible interceptors. But as the attack
planes flew deep over the Bismarck Sea, the scouts reported
no signs of the enemy. It appeared Colonel Strickland had
guessed right in plotting a detour course to the Admiralties.
The 3rd and 38th Groups had apparently avoided any
Japanese spotters on New Guinea's northern coast or on New
Britain's southern coast.

But then, at 1315 hours, within fifty miles of target, the escorting P-38's suddenly left the bombers and shot forward
like startled crows. Colonel Strickland's whole body
tightened though he saw nothing in front of him except the
diminishing P-38's. Yet, he knew instinctively that the
fighters were moving outward to give battle to enemy interceptors.

As the 3rd Group bomber formations neared Los Negros,
the crews of the bombers heard the vicious dogfight
hundreds of feet above them: a dull thunder of .50 caliber
machine guns, the echoes of whining P-38's and the squealing of Zeros, the reverberations of straining engines and
sputtering motors. And they saw the scintillating sparkles
above them: quick silver flashes across the sky, the evidence
of twisting, banking, veering aircraft locked in battle.

In Major Ed Larner's B-25, *Spook*, Joe Cardis sat nervously in his turret seat, his fingers welded to the triggers of
his .50 calibers. His gray eyes were alert, wide and bright,
darting in all directions. He saw the occasional black streaks
of distant fighters cut through the blue in straight lines, or
he saw the streaks arch across the horizon like an artist's
pencil stroke. Although some of the enemy were meeting
death, the Zeros (Mitsubishi I's) continued the struggle against

protecting P-38's to get through to the slower bombers.

The bombers now tightened their diamond patterns as a half dozen P-38's clung close to them or sped swiftly back and forth on both sides of them.

A few minutes later, the contoured land loomed before Colonel Strickland's lead plane. As the misty, graying outline turned to a hazy green, he turned to his copilot. "Look at the co-ordinate map. There's a narrow inlet on the left of our target; just south of the river."

The copilot nodded.

Moments later, the flights of B-25's and A-20's rose from their sea water height and came into the Los Negros shoreline in a thin slant. As the aircraft approached the beach, the dull echo of ack-ack boomed from the Momote Drome antiaircraft guns. The exploding pops of flak burst into small rising black clouds, hanging in midair until they dissipated.

After the planes dumped their auxiliary fuel tanks into the Bismarck Sea like duds, Strickland cried into his radio: "Scramble!"

Like trained acrobats, the first two diamonds of B-25's maneuvered into three waves, five hundred yards apart. They skimmed towards the shoreline at the fifty-foot altitude and dropped 500- and 250-pound parachute bombs atop the thick green blanket of trees near Proha Lake. Shattering explosions rattled the terrain and bursting balls of black smoke and fire mushroomed out of the brake. The eight B-25's had successfully destroyed the oil storage tanks on Los Negros.

By the time the orange balls of fire from these first waves of planes had settled to heavy smoke, curling a thousand feet upwards, the second group of B-25's reached more half-hidden oil storage tanks near Porha Lake. Here the actions were repeated. Within minutes, the same black, oily smoke rose hundreds of feet, indicating the second cluster of oil storage tanks had been destroyed.

Meanwhile, A-20's of the 3rd Group headed towards the nearly finished oil refinery. They unleashed several tons of bomb clusters leaving the refinery in shambles—a twisted, burning wreck.

When the last three A-20's unloaded their frags and skidded napalm bombs into the trees, a final burst of flame charred the area. The jungle forest between the beach and

Momote Drome was enveloped in thick black smoke. The stored oil reserves and green foliage had disappeared.

But now the 38th Group found trouble. As their B-25's zoomed over Lorengeau Drome on Manus Island and dropped their bomb clusters on a second array of oil storage tanks, they were met by thick, accurate antiaircraft fire. The storage tanks exploded as before at Porha Lake; the B-25's of the 38th Group had matched the success of the 3rd Group. But as they arched southward and out to sea, a surface gun ripped open the fuselage of one plane, causing it to spurt a trail of black smoke. The Mitchell fantailed twice and toppled into the trees beyond Lorengeau Airdrome in a fiery explosion. Flak also hit a second B-25 and the bubble turret and its gunner disappeared in the ensuing blast. But the plane remained airborne. Before the 38th Group's planes finally left the holocaust around Lorengeau Drome, another B-25 was riddled by ack-ack fire, its fuselage punctured with flak. However, this plane, too, remained aloft.

From his turret position in Major Larner's B-25, Sergeant Joe Cardis watched in horror the death of the 38th Group's B-25. He kept his fingers on the trigger of his guns, irrationally expected to ward off the distant ground fire of Lorengeau Drome with his twin fifties. But none of the ack-ack fire struck his B-25. Fortunately, the B-25's and the A-20's of the 3rd Bomb Group had met little retaliatory ground fire when they hit the storage tanks and refinery west of Porha Lake. They had come into the target area first and had missed the bulk of the antiaircraft fire that later met the 38th Bomb Group Mitchells with murderous intensity.

The raid was over in fifteen minutes and the surviving planes of the 38th Group soon fused into formation with planes of the 3rd Group. They had jelled off the Los Negros coast for the trip home. The P-38's, who themselves had strafed enemy troops in the target areas, soon joined the B-25's and A-20's. Now, the planes droned calmly southward over the Bismarck Sea, the coast of Los Negros fading behind them.

The worst seemed over, but suddenly the silver sparkles again! Enemy interceptors were screaming in from the western sky. Hamp fighters (Mitsubishi II's) had streaked out of the undamaged Lorengeau Drome to bear down on the American aircraft. The bomber formations tightened and gunners wheeled in their turrets to meet the approaching enemy fighters. The P-38's scooted westward to halt the interceptors but the Lightnings could not stop all of them. Some of the Japanese Hamps broke through the escort and lunged at the bombers like angry wasps.

Three Hamp fighters ganged up on the trailing plane of one B-25 formation, ripping its tail to shreds with a barrage of tracers. The Mitchell fell apart and its pieces plopped into the sea. The right wing aircraft of Strickland's lead flight also fell victim to Hamps when enemy fighters opened its fuselage and sliced off its right wing. The engine and gas tank exploded simultaneously. The B-25 pinwheeled downward and splashed into the sea in a sizzle of hot steam.

In another flight, a third Mitchell suffered minor damage when Hamp tracers riddled its fuselage. But the blow had cost the Japanese fighter dearly. The gunner sent a stream of .50 caliber hits into the underbelly of the enemy plane as it arched away. The Hamp burst into flames, stopped in midair, and then plunged dizzily into the sea in a splashing explosion.

Three more B-25's, including Larner's, had also suffered an assortment of hits before the main body of 35th Fighter Group and 49th Fighter Group escort planes zoomed in from the western sky to rejoin the fray. The Lightnings had shot down six Zeros in their dogfight before the bombing raid. Now the Lightning pilots shot down another six Hamps after the bombing raid and sent the rest scurrying westward. As the P-38's approached their bombers, the few Hamps still pestering the bombers zoomed away. Generally, Japanese pilots fared poorly one on one, and taking on higher odds could be suicidal against the much better trained Allied fighter pilots.

The formations headed eastward and tallied their losses. The bomb groups had lost three B-25's and suffered damage to at least six others. Three dead and several wounded airmen were aboard the damaged planes. Of the fighters, four had been lost. However, besides the dozen fighters shot down by the P-38's, a B-25 gunner had shot down one for a total of 13 kills. The score was not bad for the utter destruction of a refinery complex in the Admiralties.

Among the damaged bombers was Major Ed Larner's B-25. He had lost his right engine and was forced to feather the engine to avoid a fire that might spread to the rest of the air-craft. The major, with only one engine, was slowed to 150 knots. He radioed Colonel Strickland and told the 3rd Group commander of the damage to his aircraft.

Strickland considered the problem. He did not want to leave a damaged B-25 behind. It could fall easy victim to at-tacking Japanese fighters whom the colonel feared would swarm out of their bases at Wewak and Cape Gloucester to intercept the returning bombers. His first instinct was to slow down the entire group to 150 knots so that Larner's crip-pled B-25 could remain with the formations. But such a slow-down would run the escorting P-38's out of fuel before the fighters reached the safety of Dobodura. Further, a slow-down would offer an easier target for any further Japanese interceptors.

When Strickland failed to answer immediately, Larner knew the Third Group commander was wrestling with his conscience. Larner took the initiative.

"We'll be all right," Larner radioed Strickland. "We'll head for Wau."

"I don't know," Strickland hesitated.

But then, at 6 to 12 o'clock, north, both Colonel Strickland and Major Larner spotted the thick clouds rolling westward and southward over the Bismarck Sea. The predicted weather front had materialized.

"If we have to, we'll duck into the clouds, Colonel," Larner said. "Don't hang back on our account. Take them home." "Roger," Strickland answered reluctantly.

THE REST OF THE GROUP AND ITS escorting fighters zoomed away. Before long the formation of bombers and fighters had disappeared into the eastern sky and Major Larner and his two crewmen felt isolated as they hung above the wide expanse of the Bismarck Sea. Larner checked his chart with his copilot, Lieutenant Sal Dineo, to determine the closest route to Wau. They decided to continue eastward and then turn south above the Huon Peninsula.

Larner nursed *Spook* along for another thirty minutes when he noticed a frown on the face of his copilot, who was shifting his glance between the instrument panel and the aerial scenery beyond his cockpit window. When the major inquired, Dineo ignored him. Instead, the lieutenant took a small compass out of his pocket and stared intently at the dial.

"What's wrong?" Larner asked again.

"Our readings," Dineo said. "It's 1450 hours by my watch and the sun should be at four o'clock if we're flying east by southeast. Instead, we're closer to three o'clock. We're off by ten or fifteen degrees."

Almost as one, both airmen suspected that flak from Japanese antiaircraft fire had damaged their instrument panel. Larner and Dineo spread out a map on the copilot's lap and the lieutenant placed a T-square over it. The two men then checked the chart for two or three minutes with the compass in Dineo's hand.

Larner gasped. Instead of flying east by southeast towards the Huon Peninsula they were flying almost due east— directly into the jaws of Japanese-held New Britain. By his calculations, Larner estimated they were less than 50 miles from the Gazelle Peninsula. They were nearly 100 miles above Cape Gloucester, so they were far off course. Larner quickly altered his flight path, using the chart and his copilot's compass to lay a course for Wau.

However, Larner and Dineo had barely settled back in their cockpit when Joe Cardis called from his turret position. He reported a large formation of planes several miles to the left at nine o'clock. They were moving, almost nonchalantly, in an easterly direction.

"Something's going on," Larner said. "Why the hell are there so many, and right smack in the middle of the Bismarck Sea?"

Larner looked at the chart, but before he could take a reading Cardis' voice came blasting through the intercom: "Zekes! Three of 'em have broken off and they're comin' after us!"

Ed Larner was no coward, but he knew he was in no position to fight off three fighters with only one turret gunner. He banked the plane into a full 90-degree turn and shot upwards and northward as fast as his crippled Mitchell could move. Before the Zeros could reach the bomber's location, the B-25 had ducked into the thick cloud formations.

Larner checked his altimeter: 4800 feet. Safe enough. For the next several minutes he flew blindly through the thick clouds, hoping the Zeros would give up the pursuit. But sud-

denly he was struck by a horrible possibility: he might ram
his ship into one of the jagged shoreline peaks of the Gazelle
Peninsula. And it could happen at any second because he had
no idea how far he was from the coastline. He had to think
and act quickly. Instinctively, he knew he couldn't rise above
the thick clouds because those damn fighters might be
waiting for him. He decided to drop *under* the clouds and
take his chances by skimming above the surface of the sea.

Larner nosed his aircraft down. 4500 feet . . . 3500 . . . 2500
. . . 1500. . . . Finally, the B-25 emerged from the clouds at
close to 1,000 feet above the choppy waters of the Bismarck
Sea. Seconds later, all three crew members were staring bug-
eyed at an astonishing sight. Below the Mitchell, and only a
couple of miles distant, the vast 22-ship convoy of Admiral
Masatomi Kimura was spread out over a full square mile.
Cruisers, destroyers, tankers, transports. To the wide eyes of
Larner, Dineo, and Cardis, the armada seemed to stretch as
far as the eye could see.

"My God!" Larner croaked.

But if Ed Larner was stunned it was only for a split second.
Immediately his brain started calculating the military importance of what he was observing. He now understood why
they had seen several squadrons of enemy fighter planes in
the middle of the Bismarck Sea. The aircraft were obviously
a protective cover for the convoy. As for the convoy itself, the
major only had time for an ominous educated guess. The
Japanese could be sending a fully equipped ground force to
New Guinea, probably to reinforce their stalled troops. If
they succeeded in landing, the result would be a major disaster for the Allies. With additional men, the Japanese could
conceivably capture all of New Guinea, including Port
Moresby. And that would leave Australia open to attack.

While Larner whirred off these possibilities, the vanguard
picket of the convoy, the destroyer *Asashio*, whirled and
raced forward at full steam, her bow guns firing into the sky.
There was a burst of flak within forty yards of the B-25's tail.
The concussion bounced the Mitchell and her occupants.
Larner jerked, pulled the wheel towards him, and drove his
plane back up into the clouds until he leveled off at 4,000 feet.

Safe for the moment, and now a comfortable distance
from shoreline peaks, Larner and Dineo checked their location with their chart and compass. They both agreed the ar-

mada steaming across the Bismarck Sea was at 4.9 degrees south, 150.3 degrees east. The recent trauma of the raid on the Admiralties now seemed insignificant. With mounting excitement, Larner picked up his radio phone and called Dobodura. Forcing his voice to remain calm, he told the Dobodura operator that he had made a major discovery.

But when Larner reported his find, the sighting of a huge Japanese convoy, the base radio operator's response was less than enthusiastic. He informed Larner that a patrolling B-24 had already spotted the convoy. The Liberator crew had spotted the ships at about 1500 hours, some 40 miles northeast of the Gazelle Peninsula. Further, Fifth Air Force had immediately dispatched a flight of B-17's to intercept the convoy, but bad weather had forced the Flying Fortresses to turn back.

Still, the radio operator said, he was grateful for this latest sighting and the current location of the convoy. He thanked Major Larner and promised to relay the information to Fifth Air Force Headquarters at Port Moresby without delay.

Larner, deflated because his discovery had been secondhand, muttered an oath under his breath. Throwing a sour glance at Dineo, he banked *Spook* into a wide turn and headed for Wau. But Ed Larner would see the convoy again. To be sure, the major would be a key figure in the upcoming Operation Bismarck Sea.

Chapter Five

WHITEHEAD'S COMMITMENT

Fifth Air Force ADVON headquarters was the only multiple structure in Port Moresby. The structure, bulging on one side and sagging on the other, rose in three rickety frame levels. The building had formerly been the Port Moresby Hotel, a haven for traders, drifters, and adventurers who penetrated the jungle interior, seeking riches after the Wau gold strike. The hotel had also served as base for the ANGAU government men who spread through the island civilizing the Papuan natives.

The structure's three-sided porch along the first-floor landing was the epitome of deterioration. Its warped wooden deck was black from an eon of neglect. The picket railing leaned outward, a hazard. The plank flooring of the building's interior was equally warped from the years of dampness and neglect. Every last wall of the hotel's 20 rooms was scarred with peeling, broken, or soft plaster.

When the Fifth Air Force occupied the building in 1942, they laid new sheets of tar paper on the sloping roof and sealed the joints with quick-drying cement. And they

replaced the Doric columns of the porch with new 4x4's lest
the roof some day collapse atop one of the high-ranking officers who constantly came in and out of the building.

Though the Fifth Air Force offices in the aged hotel
generally bustled with activity, the late afternoon of 1 March
1943 saw an unusual excitement in and around the old Port
Moresby landmark. Inside, from the radio center in the old
dining hall to the chart room in a third floor suite, there was
a feverish urgency. Men, phones, typewriters, and pencils
were in constant motion. A parade of uniformed men, cor-
porals to colonels, had been running in and out of the place
for the past hour—like firemen whisking valuables from a
burning building.

In the growing dusk, the setting sun threw an orange hue
on the old building and on the crowd who milled about the
weeded grounds in front of it. A mixture of GI's, sailors, and
Australians loitered about in curiosity, drawn to the area by
the sudden upsurge of activity. Men long in the jungle
developed an instinct for suspecting crises. The crowd sought
answers, but they were brusquely ignored by those rushing
to and from the building. Each rebuff, however, only raised
more questions: Why the excitement? Had the Japanese invaded Gona or Oro Bay? Or perhaps they'd swept through
Wau? Or again moved over the Kokoda Trail? Or was it we,
the Allies, who had made a sudden move in the standoff New
Guinea campaign? Had we invaded Salamaua with our
meager ground forces?

Finally, an Australian corporal seized the arm of a
sergeant scurrying from the building. He yanked the non-
com to a stop. "Matey! 'Old up, Matey! What the bloody 'ell's
goin' on?"

"Ain't you heard?" the headquarter's airman asked in surprise.

Disgruntled faces confronted the sergeant. "We don' know
a thing, Yank," the Australian said. "We never 'ear what's
up."

"The Japs are sending an invasion fleet to New Guinea."

"Invasion!" The word sent an electric spark of fear through
the crowd.

"Last we heard, about a hundred ships," the sergeant continued. "Everything—battleships, cruisers—*everything!*"

The sergeant, like most subordinates, possessed only bits

of actual fact. He had embellished his piece of knowledge, coupled it with equally magnified pieces of information from others, and had allowed GI imagination and emotion to do the rest.

"You're jokin', Matey."

"No sir," the sergeant shook his head vigorously. "I got to get to the 43rd Bomb Group right now. They may be going out in the morning." So saying, he shook himself free of the Australian and hurried towards a jeep.

The stunned crowd fell into hurried, clamorous conversations. A few sped away, anxious to relay the astounding news to others of their units.

INSIDE THE HOTEL IN THE headquarters room behind the lobby, General Ennis Whitehead, Colonel Pappy Gunn, two Fifth Air Force staff colonels, and Brigadier General Frank Smith of the Fifth Fighter Command stood in a semi-circle around a huge map of the Bismarck Archipelago. The chart was posted on a six-by-eight-foot panel that had been nailed to a construction frame of two-by-fours, since the rotted wall behind might have collapsed from the slightest weight.

One of the colonels, an officer from Fifth Air Force G-2 (Intelligence) had been explaining the sightings to General Whitehead and General Smith. The G-2 officer pointed out that the B-24 had sighted the convoy three hours ago at 1500 hours, less than fifty miles northeast of New Britain's Gazelle Peninsula. The colonel then tapped a spot on the Bismarck Sea where Major Ed Larner had reported seeing the convoy an hour later: 4.9 degrees south, 150.3 degrees east. The two sightings, an hour apart, strongly inferred that the convoy was apparently heading for the Dampier Strait between Rooke Island and Cape Gloucester, where they could pick up fighter plane protection from Cape Gloucester at the western tip of New Britain.

Neither the B-24 patrol plane nor Major Larner had time for a thorough look at the convoy because Japanese warship gunners had quickly chased them off with antiaircraft fire. But both the B-24 and the B-25 observers had estimated the convoy at between fifteen and twenty ships, half of which appeared to be merchantmen and the other half destroyers and/or cruisers. G-2 estimated the convoy carried a fully equipped Japanese ground force division or perhaps more.

They believed the Japanese intended to fatten their Lae garrison and launch a new offensive against Wau.

"They might even be planning a landing around Buna to wrest the Dobodura airstrips," the intelligence officer expanded.

General Whitehead now turned to Pappy Gunn for an inventory of available bombers and to General Smith for an inventory of fighter planes.

"Gunn has all the figures," General Smith said.

Gunn nodded. He had already made a rough estimate of their serviceable aircraft and he referred to a clipboard he held in his hand. Although he did not have the latest figures, he did have the Fifth Air Force strength as of three days prior.

Two American fighter groups, the 35th and 49th, had a total of forty-three P-40's and thirty-five P-38's, while the Australian 9th Operational Group showed a paper strength of seventeen P-40's and 13 Beaufighters. However, neither Gunn nor General Smith could guarantee that all 108 fighter planes were in combat-ready condition. (In fact, four of the P-38's had been lost that day on the Admiralties mission.) Both Gunn and Smith agreed that even 100 or so combat-ready fighters would be poor odds against three or four hundred Zero and Hamp fighter planes the Japanese could muster against them. And in view of the two or three squadrons of fighters discovered by Major Larner over the Bismarck Sea, it appeared the Japanese intended to do just that—use all their available aircraft to protect the convoy.

"But we won't lay any of our fighters back," General Smith promised.

The Allied bomber strength, according to Pappy Gunn, was even worse. The Australian 9th Operational Group had thirteen Beaufort light bombers and six A-20's. The 3rd Bomb Group and the 38th Bomb Group had a total of thirty-three B-25's and eleven A-20's between them in the most recent tally. (Again, however, three B-25's had been lost on the Admiralties mission and several more damaged.) The 321st Heavy Bomb Squadron possessed nine B-24's and the 43rd Heavy Bomb Group had twenty-eight B-17's, the largest of any of the bomb groups. But most of the 321st's B-24's doubled as reconnaissance planes and the Liberators were not likely to be available for attacks against the convoy. Thus the Allies, at best, could not send more than a squadron or two of bombers against the convoy at once. The same was true of fighter planes. Obviously, it would be a patchwork attack force.

But if the Allied air units in New Guinea were outgunned, they made up for it in the quality of their manpower.

The 35th Fighter Group pilots had been in combat areas since May of 1942, including their veteran commander, Colonel Richard Legg. He had spent a year fighting against twice his number in dogfights, yet he and his pilots had knocked down more than a hundred Japanese fighter planes to a loss of less than a dozen of his own fighters.

The same was true of the 49th Fighter Group, who alone had thwarted the Japanese attempt to destroy Darwin after the fall of Java. The 49th pilots had knocked down half the attacking bombers in several attacks on Darwin, thus saving an invasion of Australia on the northwest coast. In every dogfight, the 49th pilots, under the command of Colonel Bob Morrissey, had shot down four times as many planes as they had lost themselves.

The Australian 9th Operational Group, composed of a motley array of fighter planes and light bombers, had served in the New Guinea jungles since the beginning of the war. Their bomber crews had never known a day when they did not meet a swarm of enemy fighters on a bombing run. Yet, these Aussie air crews never turned back in attacking troop concentrations, airfields, harbor installations, or shipping.

The 43rd Bomb Group consisted mostly of B-17 bomber crews from the old 19th Bomb Group who had lived with the daily prospect of death or capture during the retreat from the Philippines. The crews had been absorbed into the newly established 43rd in the fall of 1942. Since then, 43rd airmen had conducted more than 400 sorties in long-range missions against Japanese East Indies bases. Under the capable command of Colonel Roger Ramey, the 43rd had become a most experienced and effective heavy bomb group.

The 321st Heavy Bomb Squadron, badly understrengthed in both planes and men, served mostly as reconnaissance planes. They had been detached from Hawaii and sent to New Guinea a few months before. They had made a creditable record thus far, sinking numerous Japanese barges and destroying enemy installations.

The 38th and 3rd Bomb Groups had been the workhorses of the Southwest Pacific air campaigns, having absorbed many of the Philippine air veterans from the old 27th Bomb Group, now disbanded. These medium bomb groups had become proficient in low-level bomb strikes against airstrips, enemy troop concentrations, and shipping. They had learned to use every improvised attack technique devised by the remarkable Pappy Gunn: strafing guns, napalms, parachute bombs and, for the 3rd Group, the new skip bomb. The pilots and gunners of these light bomb groups had never known a day's rest and rarely returned from a mission without successful results. In the person of Bob Strickland, commander of 3rd Group, Fifth Air Force had a sharp, fearless group leader.

So if General Ennis Whitehead's Command was inferior in numbers to the Japanese air force, he felt confident that the versatility and experience of the battle-tested veterans in his air units would compensate for the difference. However, Whitehead sobered a bit when he reflected that his men were up against a double-edged sword. They not only would have to go up against enemy pilots, but also test the skills of Japanese sailors, men who had tasted the sweet wine of victory while serving under the "Eel of the Pacific," Admiral Masatomi Kimura.

Despite the small number of serviceable aircraft available, Whitehead took direct action. "We'll suspend all other bombing missions and concentrate on this convoy." He looked at the colonel from G-2. "Are we tracking the convoy now?"

"A B-24 was shadowing the ships and their course," the colonel replied, "but it lost the armada because of heavy cloud cover. Still," the colonel placed his finger on the map, "we know the convoy was moving at seven to nine knots. So we can figure they'll be on the western side of the Gazelle Peninsula by morning. We can also assume that they won't come within range of our medium or light bombers until they leave the Dampier Strait. And that should be sometime late tomorrow afternoon." He jabbed his forefinger at the map, emphasizing his point.

"How can we be sure they're going through the Dampier

Strait?" Pappy Gunn asked, nodding at the map.

"With a base full of fighters only a stone's throw from Cape Gloucester?" the intelligence officer said with a grin.

General Whitehead looked at Colonel Gunn and General Smith. "Can we send out our heavies at dawn with P-38's?"

Smith squeezed his face. The P-38's would need auxiliary fuel tanks to range that far into the Bismarck Sea. If the fighters met interceptors before they reached the convoy, they'd have difficulty in maneuvering with the bulky belly tanks. However, Smith agreed that they needed to hit the convoy as soon as possible and he assured Whitehead that his P-38's would go. They would simply drop their belly tanks if they hit Japanese interceptors before they contacted the convoy.

Pappy Gunn said there would be no problems to ready the heavy bombers.

General Whitehead now ordered the 43rd Bomb Group to take off the next morning, a decision all but expected, since the 43rd had 28 available B-17 long-range bombers. Whitehead also told Smith to send out the P-38's of both the 49th and 35th Fighter Groups to escort the Flying Fortresses. The B-17's should carry 1000- and 500-pound bombs, with some of the aircraft carrying bomb clusters. The P-38's would carry auxiliary fuel tanks.

"I'd like them over target by 0700," Whitehead finished.

Before anyone could speak again, a staff colonel entered the meeting room with a sheaf of paper in his hand. He told Whitehead that three PBY's of the Australian 16th Reconn-Rescue Squadron at Oro Bay had left their base at 1700 to seek out the convoy. The Catalinas had found the armada skirting the northwest tip of the Gazelle Peninsula and it appeared the armada was definitely heading westward through the Bismarck Sea to the Dampier Strait. At their present speed the convoy would probably reach the Dampier Strait sometime late tomorrow, so there was a possibility that medium and light bombers could sortie against the ships then. However, Cape Gloucester was on the Dampier Strait and the bombers could expect plenty of fighter interceptors.

Whitehead nodded, absorbing the information.

"The PBY's will be working in relays," the colonel continued. "A new three-plane flight will replace the old every couple of hours. They'll track the convoy all night. We'll have a direct radio band with the Cats to our headquarters here in Port Moresby."

"Fine, fine," Whitehead nodded again.

A moment later, a sergeant rushed into the meeting room. He carried a weather report. "Sir, weather observation says that dense clouds are sweeping over the entire Bismarck Archipelago, getting thicker all the time. As of 1800, estimated ceiling was no more than 2500 feet."

Both Whitehead and Pappy Gunn grimaced. B-17's were not designed for low-level bombing; they generally needed at least 5,000 feet of altitude for maximum effectiveness. However, Whitehead made a hurried call to Colonel Roger Ramey, commander of the 43rd Bomb Group. He told the colonel that his unit would be the first Fifth Air Force unit to hit the convoy. He warned Ramey, however, that the weather forecast was bad and that a cloud front might close in in the Bismarck Sea by morning.

"We'll be okay," Ramey said.

"We'd like you off by 0500 and over target by 0700," Whitehead said. "You'll have P-38's for cover from the 49th and 35th Fighter Groups, though you won't have too many of them. And as I said, visibility might be poor. The last report says that ceiling is down to 2500 feet."

"We want 'em," Colonel Ramey said. "We want 'em bad and we'll hit from sea level if necessary. We'll use parachute frag clusters if we have to. Just give us a weather report at 0400 before we load up, so we'll know what to use."

General Whitehead grinned, satisfied, as he hung up the phone. He then told the sergeant from weather observation to make certain that both he and the 43rd Bomb Group received reports on the weather front at least every hour. Whitehead then told his staff colonel to notify the tracking PBY's to also report weather conditions and the location of the convoy every hour. Next, Whitehead turned to Pappy Gunn. "I want all our other bomb groups on alert. We may be sending out the 43rd at 0500, but they won't be the only group that goes out tomorrow."

"They'll be ready," Gunn promised.

Finally, Whitehead turned to General Smith. "I want all fighter units on the ready, too."

"They'll be set," Smith said.

Whitehead now sighed. "Okay, I guess we've done all we can."

When his staff left his office, General Whitehead cleared his desk of paper work and sipped at another cup of coffee as he studied the map on his wall. Before the coffee cup was half empty, the phone rang. The call was from an agitated Lieutenant General George Kenney at Fifth Air Force Headquarters in Brisbane. Kenney was bursting with curiosity for he had heard all kinds of rumors about the Japanese convoy, reports that had already spread through Australia in a mixture of fact, fiction, and exaggeration.

"What the hell's going on up there?" Kenney wanted to know. "We've got figures of ten and a 100 shiploads of Japanese troops heading for Lae. What's the story?"

If anyone had a more irascible temper than General Whitehead, it was George C. Kenney, Whitehead's superior. Kenney, a 20-year veteran bomber pilot, had shown a phenomenal rise in the Army Air Corps. In 1941 he had been jumped from the rank of Lieutenant Colonel to Brigadier General and placed in command of the Fourth Air Force, stateside. He had done a remarkable job with the Fourth in training them for strategic bombardment. As a result, when the Fifth Air Force was organized in the fall of 1942, Kenney had been personally selected by General MacArthur from a dozen air corps generals to head up the new combat air force.

Kenney, in turn, had recognized the worth of Ennis Whitehead, and he had selected Whitehead as his deputy commander to head the Fifth Air Force ADVON combat command in Port Moresby. Thus, despite Kenney's curtness, Whitehead had little or no fear of him.

General Whitehead readily admitted he should have called Fifth Air Force in Brisbane before this. However, he had been busy every minute since they had sighted the convoy at midafternoon today. First of all, the convoy was not a hundred ships but between fifteen and twenty ships, according to the latest estimate. G-2 calculated the ships were probably carrying a fully equipped division of ground troops and perhaps a little more. Whitehead further told Kenney that reconn planes had the convoy under minute-by-minute surveillance so they knew the armada's location at all times.

As of now, Fifth Air Force in Port Moresby planned dawn air strikes against the convoy. Subsequent air strikes would follow through the day.

"Keep me informed, Ennis, keep me informed!" Kenney ordered. "And don't screw this one up like the one in January. If that convoy reaches Lae, there'll be be hell to pay. Too many wheels are calling the air corps useless and we don't want to give them more ammunition."

"This is one convoy that won't get away," Whitehead assured Kenney. "We sighted them early, and it'll take two or three days before they can make Lae. We'll finish them off by then."

"I damn well hope so," Kenney answered.

After the call from General Kenney, Whitehead took a deep breath. He was not one hundred percent certain he could deliver, and he suffered second thoughts about his impetuous promise to destroy the convoy. He knew the adeptness of Japanese helmsmen in avoiding aerial bomb attacks. He also knew that heavy fighter cover had thwarted the first mission against the smaller Japanese convoy in January. True, there'd be hell to pay if Fifth Air Force let this huge convoy get away. The arrival of a fresh, fully equipped Japanese division could truly break the stalemate in New Guinea in the enemy's favor.

Whitehead looked at the map of the Bismarck Archipelago behind him and tapped the location of Dampier Strait. They had to kill the convoy there, before they could make the run across the Solomon Sea with a skyful of Japanese air cover from Madang, Lae, Wewak, and Cape Gloucester. But how the hell could he neutralize these Japanese air bases with his minimal complement of combat-ready planes and still use his planes to destroy the convoy? He'd need to send out anything that could fly as soon as the convoy reached the Dampier Strait. However, the Fifth Air Force ADVON commander was apprehensive and uncertain. His stomach suddenly felt sour. He had lost his appetite for food and that night he drank black coffee for dinner.

DURING THE LATE AFTERNOON of 1 March 1943, the Bismarck Sea was hardly conducive to a pleasant sea voyage. Thick thunderclouds overhead, white, gray, or near black, had left the panoramic view beyond the convoy dark and gloomy. The usually sparkling waters had changed to an angry, ominous gray. The weather, nurtured by blowing winds in a slight gale, had left the air damp from a misty rain. The same winds had also churned up breakers that swirled across the surface of the sea in thick, erratic thrusts, the breakers surfing in whatever direction the changing winds sent them. Whitecaps offered the only bright spot in the otherwise dark, dull afternoon.

The steaming ships heaved and listed as they struggled through the thick, unfriendly sea. Aboard the flag cruiser *Shirayuki*, Admiral Masatomi Kimura stood next to the port railing on the semicircle of deck just fore of the wheelhouse. He clung tenaciously to the railing, swaying backward or forward as the big cruiser rolled in the swollen sea. The admiral's face was soaked from the ocean spray that shot over the deck whenever the cruiser slapped the water against a heavy swell, or whenever slanting drops of rain whooshed across the bridge. But Kimura remained motionless on the bridge, almost like the stationary searchlight next to him, as he stared intently into the foul weather before him.

The discovery of the convoy had failed to alter his sober face or the blank look in his eyes. Thus, in his calm, relaxed stance, Kimura offered an abrupt contrast to the bouncy General Whitehead. The admiral could almost be mistaken for a tourist on a tranquil sea voyage.

Three hours had passed since the B-24 had dipped out of the clouds and discovered the convoy. Nearly two hours had passed since the sailors had heard the low drone of B-17's far above the clouds, searching futilely for the armada. Now the sailors intermittently saw or heard the PBY's who were tracking them. Every officer and man in the Lae Resupply Convoy knew their position had been relayed to Port Moresby. Yet, Kimura had done nothing. He had not changed a single block of the *hochi* pattern. He had not altered course to hide among the many coves along the Gazelle Peninsula. Instead, the admiral had continued the same westerly course in the open Bismarck Sea. All he had done since the convoy's discovery was to ask for weather reports.

A half hour earlier, he had ordered his staff to secure all ships by 1700. The last order had stunned his subordinates. They were under constant surveillance. Shouldn't they remain at battle stations? But no one had protested to the admiral about this puzzling set of orders.

Kimura's executive officer, Captain Yukata Tishayuna, reflected the silent concern of thousands of others in the 22-ship convoy. Though impatient with doubt, he stood silently behind his poker-faced admiral in stiff erectness. He neither pressed Kimura for the admiral's thoughts nor requested answers to his own burning questions.

"Captain Tishayuna," Kimura finally spoke.

"Yes, Honorable Admiral." The captain, grateful for the address from Kimura, quickly stepped forward.

"The latest weather report."

Captain Tishayuna snapped his fingers and two sailors disappeared quickly from the bridge. A moment later they returned and handed Tishayuna a slip of paper. The captain read: "Dense cloud cover continues to expand throughout the Bismarck Archipelago. Depth of nimbus clouds now estimated at 3,000 feet; visibility, 1,500 feet."

"Thank you, Captain."

The short conversation gave Tishayuna courage, and the subordinate's burning curiosity finally overcame his submissiveness. "Admiral, unless we alter our two-five-eight present course, will we not be on the open sea all the way to the Dampier Strait?"

"We do not go to the Dampier Strait," the admiral said.

The subordinate blinked. His face cracked as emotional lines raced across his cheek. "But Admiral Kimura, should we not at least seek shelter at Cape Gloucester? Surely, if the Americans attack us on the open sea, especially at our slow speed—"

"We do not go to Cape Gloucester " the admiral repeated brusquely. "Maintain present speed of nine knots. Then, the admiral stepped back from the bridge railing. "I go to my quarters now. Ask Captain Watanabe to see me at once."

"Yes, sir," Tishayuna bowed. As Kimura left the bridge, Captain Tishayuna stared dubiously after him, allowing the slanting rain to pelt his face. By morning dozens of American bombers would be seeking the armada. Was not the shelter of Cape Gloucester, where dozens of Zeros could protect them, more feasible than the open sea?

Only Kimura's reputation enabled Tishayuna to regain his composure. He remembered that Kimura had only recently carried the 102nd Brigade safely to Lae. He remembered that only Kimura had brought reinforcements into the Solomons with minimum losses. Captain Yukata Tishayuna must simply trust his commander.

Chapter Six

THE EEL SLIPS AWAY

By 1943, the Dobodura air base on New Guinea's northeast coast was the closest air base to Japanese-held territory. Located at the foot of the Owen Stanley Range in northern Papua, New Guinea, it resembled a T. Bulldozers had first leveled the old runways of the Japanese. They had then hewn a new 3,000-yard bomber runway, east and west, and a new 2,000-yard fighter runway, north and south. Two taxi strips paralleled the bomber runway, one for the bombers and one for the fighter planes.

On one side of the T, dozens of dirt mound revetments sheltered the P-40's, P-38's, and P-39's of the 49th and 35th Fighter Groups. The B-25's and A-20's of the 38th and 3rd Bomb Groups rested in dispersal revetments on the other side of the T. On the eastern edge of the fighter runway, the Australian 9th Operational Group occasionally parked its Beauforts and Beaufighters when they came north from Tufi to join American air groups on a bomb run.

Line shacks, repair shacks, communications tents, operation huts, and thatched-roof tool sheds were interspersed among the revetments. The Japanese, chagrined and disturbed by this growing menace to their bases in the Bismarck Archipelago, could not ignore the growing air base complex. They regularly sent their Betty and Sally bombers from Lae and New Britain to neutralize the growing Dobodura. But, the Americans housed their squadron campsites, ammunition dumps, and bomb stockpiles deep under the surrounding jungle trees, out of sight and at least a mile or more from the open airstrips. Thus hidden, Japanese air strikes were generally ineffective, for bulldozers could quickly repair bomb craters in the airstrips themselves.

Dobodura was really a part of the Buna-Gona area on the south shore of the Solomon Sea across from Japanese-held New Britain. Before the war, Buna had been nothing more than a series of coconut plantations along the northern shoreline of Papua, New Guinea. The area had no roads, no resources, and no population except for a few hundred Papuan natives. Furthermore, the Buna-Gona area did not include a harbor. In fact, because of dangerous offshore reefs, the only access to the area was by flat barges and native fishing boats.

Why then, did the Buna-Gona area, 200 miles south of the excellent seaport at Lae, become a prize for both the Allies and Japanese? The answer lay in the flats of Dobodura, just beyond the coconut groves that stretched along the rugged coast of the Solomon Sea. The flats were ideal for airfield construction and both sides knew that air bases at Dobodura would enable the occupants to control the southern approaches of the Bismarck Archipelago.

Just as the Allies by 1943 had singled out Rabaul as their chief hazard in the Southwest Pacific, so too the Japanese considered the Buna-Gona-Dobodura complex as the principal hazard to their operations in the Southwest Pacific.

The Japanese had initially attempted to take Port Moresby in an amphibious invasion from Rabaul, several hundred miles away. The attempt failed in the abortive Battle of the Coral Sea, wherein the Japanese invasion force, vastly overestimating the strength of Allied forces, withdrew to New Britain after losing several ships. Imperial headquarters had then decided that amphibian route was simply too far away from land-based supply and air support. They decided to take Port Moresby by land.

The Japanese successfully landed 5,000 troops at Buna on July 21, 1942, against minor Allied air strikes by eight bombers and then fighter planes. The Allied strikes did damage a Japanese troop transport, but the Americans had lost two of their precious fighter planes and suffered damage to several of their even more precious bombers.

The capture of Buna gave the Japanese a strong foothold in Papua from which their bombers and fighters could fly the short 80-mile distance across the Owen Stanley Range and reduce the Allied base at Port Moresby by aerial bombardments. Moreover, Buna offered a staging area for ground troops to strike out at Port Moresby over the Owen Stanleys, using the Kokoda Trail.

The operation to capture Port Moresby and thus drive the Allies from New Guinea began in early August, 1942, but stubborn Australian ground troops with the aid of the American 32nd Division's 128th Regiment of infantry, stalled the Japanese drive at Kokoda, high in the Owen Stanley Mountains. Then, with the invasion of Guadalcanal, the Japanese shifted their efforts to the Solomons, allowing the Allies to seize the initiative in New Guinea. The Australian and American troops pushed the Japanese down the Owen Stanleys, north, to the Buna-Gona area. Here, the bitter fight for Buna went on for several weeks. Finally, when American C-47 transport planes dropped paratroopers on the Dobodura flats on November 19, the battle swung in the Allies' favor. Japanese troops who did not evacuate in barges were slaughtered in the ravaged coconut groves or on the bloodied beaches.

The heavy fighting at Buna had stripped a two-mile width of seacoast from Buna to Gona of jungle trees. Battered coconut groves had been flattened for several square miles. Huge bomb and shell craters, already miniature swamps and infested with insect larva, dotted the shorn terrain like huge pegboards. Sunken barges, rusted weapons, brush-engulfed bunkers, and the occasional remains of a decomposed enemy soldier completed the legacy of the vicious Buna campaign.

The thunder of airlifted artillery, the roar of supporting planes, and the resolution of exhausted Allied troops had not only destroyed the determined Japanese Forces but had also chased the remnants of wildlife into the uncertain mountain jungles. Still, Fifth Air Force looked eagerly at the Dobodura

Adm. Jinichi Kasaka, commander 11th Air Fleet, was to provide air cover for the Lae Resupply Convoy; Gen. Hitoshi Imamura *(bottom left)* was commander of 8th Area Forces, MacArthur's counterpart; and the convoy's commander was Adm. Masatomi Kimura *(bottom right)*, the "Eel of the Pacific."

On New Guinea, Gen. Toru Okabe *(top left)*, commander 102nd Infantry Brigade, waited for help before launching another assault on Wau; Gen. Hatazo Adachi *(top right)*, commander 18th Army in New Guinea, sailed with reinforcements aboard convoy; Adm. Gunichi Mikawa *(right)*, commander 8th Fleet, promised Kimura naval support but never delivered.

**Col. Hato Shinohara
(*sitting, 3rd from left*),
commander 7th Fighter
Squadron, whose pilots
failed to stop Allied skip
bombers; at left, one of
his aircraft, a Hamp,
splashes into the
Bismarck Sea.**

Official U.S. Air Force Photo

Parachute bombs, set to explode a few feet above ground, float down on Japanese installation at Lae, New Guinea.

Official U.S. Air Force Photo

Japanese air facility at Lae, a primary target of Allied bombers and fighters during Bismarck action.

Official U.S. Air Force Photo

Low-level reconnaissance photo of Lae, detailing topography and damage inflicted by Allied aircraft.

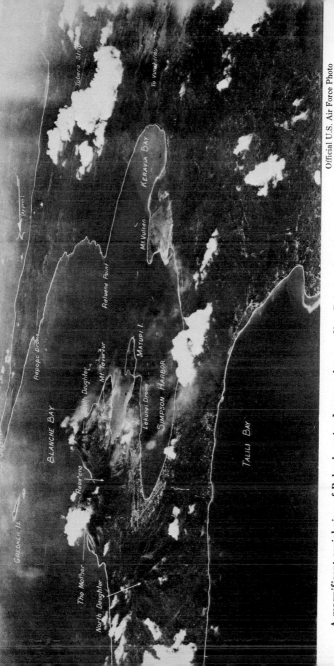

Official U.S. Air Force Photo

A magnificent aerial view of Rabaul, major Japanese base on New Britain, showing topography and harbor facilities.

Official U.S. Air Force Photo

These Zero fighters were caught by **Allied bombers at Lae,** as they attempted to refuel during **Bismarck action.**

plains, envisioning what could be built there.

"That's where we'll build our airstrips," General George Kenney said after an inspection of the area. "I want a long one that will accommodate our bombers as well as our fighters."

In early January, 1943, construction engineers and their heavy equipment moved into Buna by shallow draft barges because of the reefs off the coast. The engineers did not dawdle long on the devastated terrain. Their bulldozers soon scooped their way from the coast, cutting a four-mile road from the beaches to the flats of Dobodura. Here, they uprooted trees, squashed thick brush, filled swampy marshes, and leveled the ravaged Japanese airstrip. They then constructed their two airstrips. At construction's end, heavily laden six-by-six trucks daily crawled over the dirt road from Buna to the Dobodura flats. They brought food, ammunition, bombs, and other supplies and equipment to the air units that now occupied the base. By February, 1943, Dobodura was the biggest Allied air base in the Southwest Pacific, housing two bomb groups, two fighter groups, and assorted military reconnaissance and air transport units.

ON THE EVENING OF 1 MARCH 1943, the sun was setting over the jungle trees of Dobodura when Major Ed Larner walked into the 90th Squadron communications shack south of the bomber runway. Inside, the radio operator was twisting dials on a metal complex as he monitored reports between search planes and Fifth Air Force headquarters, ADVON, in Port Moresby. Several officers and enlisted men huddled about the operator, including Lt. Dineo and Sergeant Cardis.

The two felt a particular interest in the garble coming over the air waves, since they had seen the school of vessels in the Bismarck Sea. For the copilot the big convoy raised the question of another dangerous mission. For the young gunner, Joe Cardis, the armada offered yet another experience in aerial warfare.

"Sergeant," Larner asked the radioman, "have they verified the makeup of that convoy yet?"

"No sir," the sergeant answered. "The PBY's have been over the area for quite a while but they haven't said."

The long-range PBY's, from the Australian 16th Reconn-

Rescue Squadron, had arrived over the Bismarck Sea more than an hour ago. The Catalinas, designated Fly-by 1, Fly-by 2, and Fly-by 3, had thus far only reported the convoy's speed, location, and course. The observers were sending messages directly to Port Moresby as well as to their own headquarters in Oro Bay. However, the radio shacks of every Allied unit in Papua, including Larner's 90th Squadron, had eagerly monitored any messages from the PBY search planes. Major Larner had only been in the radio shack a few minutes when a new message came through from the Australian search planes.

" 'Igh Point, 'Igh Point, this is Fly-by 2, Fly-by 2," a garbled voice reported to Fifth Air Force in Port Moresby. "Are you reading me, 'Igh Point?"

"We read you, Fly-by 2," a heavy voice responded.

"The convoy's a big one. Covering 'alf the Bismarck Sea, she is."

"Complement! Can you give us the complement?"

"Enemy vessels at 9.5 east, 4.9 degrees south. Speed still at eight knots. A bit slow, Mate."

"Complement! What's the complement?"

"Bearing the same as before. Still two-four-six—west by southwest."

Admiral Masatomi Kimura had apparently decided to change course, and he was now on a bearing of west by southwest towards the Dampier Strait.

"Fly-by 1 and Fly-by 2 confirm course and direction," a garbled Australian voice came over the transmitter.

Meanwhile the communications officer looked at Major Larner. "Do you think we'll use the skip bomb?"

"I don't know," Larner answered.

The communications officer nodded, but the mention of skip bombs sent a chill through the marrow of Sal Dineo. The lieutenant again remembered the tragedy of Merrick Bay and the near disaster over the Admiralties only a few hours ago. If limited ground fire could pummel the dangerous low-level air strike, what would the murderous ack-ack guns of cruisers do? Dineo retreated slightly from the radio.

"Goddam it, Fly-by, what's the complement?" The heavy voice from Port Moresby now cursed angrily.

" 'Old on, 'Igh Point, 'old on," the voice from Fly-by 2 answered. "We're givin' a look now."

There was a long pause as the PBY's began the count of the convoy's makeup.

"Fly-bys 1 and 3." The garbled voice of Fly-by 2 again came over the radio. "Take stock from starboard; we're takin' port."

"This is Fly-by 1. We're moving to starboard now, Fly-by 2."

The heavy voice of High Point at Port Moresby broke irritably into the radio band again. "This is High Point. Hurry up with that count. How the hell many ships have they got in that convoy and what kind are they?"

"In a minute, 'Igh Point, in a minute."

For the next few minutes only static came over the radio. And, while the operator fingered the dials frantically to pick up the observers again, the communications officer turned to the 90th Squadron commander. "We'll have them back soon, Major. What's the word? Who's going out?"

"The 43rd is going in at dawn with P-38's from the 49th and 35th giving them cover. We'll be going in too, just as soon as those ships come into range. I guess everybody in New Guinea will go in eventually."

And Major Larner was correct.

EVER SINCE WORD OF THE CONVOY reached New Guinea, every American and Australian air unit in Papua had exploded into feverish action. At the Dobodura air base, American combat crews of the 38th Bomb Group had been going over potential bombing patterns. At the airstrips, their ground crews were loading 500 and 250 pounders into the Mitchells. Other ground technicians were testing armament, electrical systems, engine complexes, and radio equipment.

In another revetment area, the ground crews of the 3rd Bomb Group were similarly placing 500- and 250-pound bombs into the bellies of the group's B-25's and A-20's. Here, too, technicians checked out engines, electrical systems, and radio systems. Other maintenance crews were repairing flak damage on several of the 90th Squadron's Mitchells so that every available B-25 would be ready for combat.

A swarm of mechanics were frantically replacing the right engine and cowling of Ed Larner's plane, *Spook*, for there was no way the major would miss the opportunity to attack the convoy threatening Allied positions in New Guinea.

During the same cloudy evening, across the Owen Stanley hump in Port Moresby, ordnance men were loading thousand pounders into the huge bomb bays of the 43rd Bomb Group's B-17's. Other men were loading the 50-caliber belts into the assorted machine gun positions—in the nose, the belly, turret, and fuselage. The group's eleven-man crews, meanwhile, sat attentively in a huge double tent serving as briefing room. They listened as Colonel Roger Ramey, commander of the 43rd, outlined the strategy for the first strike at 0700.

Less than a mile away, the heavy bomber crews of the 321st Squadron were also conducting a briefing session. General Whitehead had decided to use the B-24 Liberators against the convoy rather than on reconnaissance, since the Aussie PBY's were doing a creditable job in tracking the convoy. The 321st would follow the B-17's against the convoy, hitting from whatever altitude they could at about 0800 hours.

Crews of the 321st worked just as feverishly as the ground crews of the 43rd Group. They armed the B-24's to the teeth: bomb bays jammed with half-ton bombs; every gun, in every gunnery position, fitted with fully loaded 50-caliber machine gun belts, with reserve belts on the fuselage deck. The heavy bomber units knew that Zeros and Hamps might swarm all over them and they'd need every gunner and every round of ammunition to ward them off.

Greasemonkeys were checking out engines, fuel lines, lubrication points. Radiomen checked intercoms and outside radios. Finally, electricians made certain the instruments and dials and other electrical systems were in good working order.

At Tufi, Australian ground crews of the 9th Operational Group similarly checked engines or electrical systems and loaded bombs and machine guns on their A-20's and Beauforts.

But while air units prepared feverishly in Dobodura, Port Moresby, and Tufi, non-crews were jammed around unit radios absorbing every word on the movement of the big Japanese convoy. Those in the 90th Squadron radio shack were an example of these curious men.

The garbled voice of the Australian PBY pilot broke

through the static. "This is Fly-by 2, Fly-by 2. Give an ear. Stock secured: two cruisers, eight destroyers, six transports, four cargos and two oilers. That's the bloody lot, Mates."

"How about confirmation?" the heavy voice from Port Moresby shot back. "Fly-by 1 and Fly-by 3, can you confirm?"

"Fly-by 3 confirms, 'Igh Point," a new voice rasped over the radio. "Two cruisers, eight destroyers, six transports, four cargos and two oilers."

"My God!" one of the enlisted men in the 90th Squadron radio shack gasped. "Six transports! That could mean a whole division. Maybe more!"

"Fly-by 3 again confirms: 22 vessels, 'Igh Point, 22. Still tracking. Target now at 148 east, 5.8 south. Course still at two-four-six."

The men in the 90th Squadron radio shack suddenly grew silent, tense. Every airman here knew the consequences if the Japanese could reinforce Lae. Dobodura was already a major target area for Japanese air units and step two would obviously include an attempt to recapture the Buna-Gona area and the Dobodura air base. Only a battalion of the 128th Regiment and two companies of the Australian 7th Division were stationed here. Worse, these few ground troops were still sapped from the Buna campaign. They could not ward off a division of fresh, fully equipped Japanese troops. The hundreds of airmen and service troops around Dobodura had only minimal infantry training and would be no match against crack Japanese ground forces.

Further, the American navy was still binding its wounds from the Solomons campaign. They could offer no serious resistance to the powerful Japanese naval units that still roamed freely throughout the Bismarck Archipelago.

When static again interrupted the radio reports from the Aussie reconn pilots, Major Ed Larner sighed and stepped out of the stuffy communication tent. He inhaled the cool night air and looked up at the heavy nimbus formations. The dark overcast was lower now, racing across the sky as though seeking a resting place. But the dense clouds found no resting place over the flat marshlands of Dobodura.

NEITHER DID THE DISTANT REACHES of these same dense clouds find any resting place over the Bismarck Sea. From the bridge of the *Shirayuki*, Admiral Kimura squinted at the darkness around him and observed the thick overcasts float southward unabated. The dark clouds also whirled downward, as though trying to snare the pagoda masts of the Japanese cruiser. Only far to the west could the admiral still see evidence of the sky, a dark orange from the setting sun. After Kimura stared once more at the dense clouds overhead, he nodded to himself and turned to Captain Yukata Tishayuna.

"At what bearing are we now?"

"On the same course of two-four-six," the convoy's executive officer answered. The admiral had earlier ordered a change in course towards the Dampier Strait, satisfying Tishayuna. The change had made the executive officer more confident and relaxed.

"How distant are we from the Dampier Strait?"

"At our reduced speed, not until morning."

"The observation planes have long enough amused themselves," Kimura said. "So too have our patient gunners waited too long. Tell the captain to open fire."

Tishayuna frowned. Why expend ammunition on spy planes? The Allies knew they were heading for the Dampier Strait. But he did not question the order. "Yes, Admiral Kimura."

The PBY's, dark globs in the early night, suddenly shuddered from the murderous barrage of 5" and 3" pom-pom concussions. The abrupt, accurate ack-ack fire quickly shredded Fly-by 1. A dozen metal fragments tumbled into the murky sea. Seconds later, Fly-by 2 met a similar fate as a 5" burst of shrapnel flak tore open the PBY's fat belly. A fiery explosion whooshed through the fuselage and the flaming plane arched into the sea like a bloated shooting star.

Fly-by 3, alertly or luckily, hoisted itself into the low-hanging nimbus cover and miraculously escaped the lethal barrage of antiaircraft fire. The Catalina pilot, cognizant of the angry swarms of Zeke fighters that might be waiting above the clouds, even in the darkness, leveled the big reconnaissance plane at 4,000 feet, deep inside the safety of the clouds.

Kimura waited two minutes. Then: "Alter course to two-five-eight bearing."

"Two-five-eight!" Captain Yukata Tishayuna cried. "But

Admiral, such an altered course is almost directly south. Would we not fail to reach the Dampier Strait by morning?"

"True," the admiral said.

Tishayuna did not answer.

"And make maximum speed—twelve knots."

"Twelve knots? But Admiral, can the heavily laden cargo vessels maintain such a speed?"

Kimura did not answer immediately. Instead, he left Tishayuna waiting while he raised his field glasses and scanned the sea. First, Kimura studied the horizon, where the setting sun and orange glow had now disappeared into darkness. Finally, he lowered his glasses, braced himself against the railing, and stared at the open sea. Without turning, he answered the concerned Tishayuna.

"Captain, soon will the west be as black as the east. The enemy will expect us to be in the Dampier Strait by morning, for they have seen us on such a course for several hours. But they will not find us there. For two hours our vessels have sailed on reduced speed and so they can increase speed for twenty knots or so without difficulty. When next the enemy seeks us out, Captain, we will be safely within the dark coves of Kimbo Bay, west of the Gazelle Peninsula. They will find only emptiness in the Dampier Strait or at Cape Gloucester or wherever they care to search. We shall remain in Kimbo Bay until fortune offers us the opportunity to continue our journey without being under the eyes of their reconnaissance."

A smile lit the face of the Lae Resupply Convoy executive officer. "Only from you, Honorable Kimura, could come such cunning and wisdom."

THE SUDDEN HEATED CHATTER BURSTING out of the 90th Squadron communications tent shook Ed Larner from his quiet meditation. He raced back inside. "What happened?"

"They knocked out a couple of the Catalinas," the communications officer answered.

". . . off starboard of convoy. Repeat: both Fly-by 1 and Fly-by 2 lost." The garbled voice rattled in horror now. "Fly-by 1 and Fly-by 2 down from flak. We're at altitude 4.0, inside cloud cover. We'll attempt new tracking in 'alf an hour."

The men in the radio shack had stiffened in horror as the radioman waited frantically for more reports. Then a voice

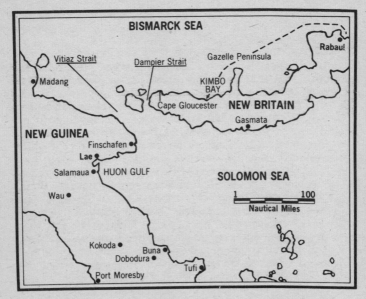

Map 3: Convoy evades Allies in sheltered lagoon off Kimbo Bay.

came from Fifth Air Force, a heavy voice pitched with urgency. "This High Point. Fly-bys 4, 5, and 6 on the way to bearing 148, 5.8. They'll take up the search."

About thirty minutes later, the pilot of the surviving PBY from the 16th Australian Reconn-Rescue Squadron cautiously dipped out of the clouds. The pilot saw nothing. "Read me, 'Igh Point, this is Fly-by 3. No sign of the convoy. Repeat: no sign of the convoy. We're at bearing 147.9, 5.9. No convoy. Continuing search on bearing two-four-six."

At his desk in Port Moresby, General Ennis Whitehead mulled over the latest reports. Since late afternoon every Fifth Air Force unit in Papua had been making feverish preparations to attack the convoy and now it was lost—at least temporarily. Whitehead glanced in disgust at the map behind him and then looked anxiously at one of his staff colonels.

The aide spoke. "Two flights of P-38's from the 35th Fighter Group are on the way to reconnoiter the area. They should be there in half an hour. They might pick up the convoy quicker because they can move faster and cover more ground than the PBY's.

Whitehead only frowned.

"We've set up a direct band with them," the aide continued, "same as we have with the PBY's. We'll keep those search planes out all night, if necessary."

The general nodded but squirmed in his chair and tapped his fingers disconcertedly on his desk. Until they again found the convoy, Whitehead could only wait. He would wait impatiently as would Colonel Morrissey of the 49th Fighter Group and Colonel Ramsey of the 43rd Bomb Group.

And not only airmen waited anxiously for a new sighting of the convoy. In the small infantry encampments at Buna, GI's of the 32nd Infantry Division waited and listened. And at their jungle camps in Oro Bay, the Australian Diggers of the 9th Division milled about apprehensively. At Wau they stiffened most of all. In their sandbag pits on the eight o'clock watch, Aussies peered tensely into the dark gloom of jungle before them. The Kanga Force most personally recognized the importance of the Japanese convoy.

The enemy, too, waited. Every Japanese soldier—those left in Rabual, those in Lae, those in the other bases of the Bismarck Archipelago. They knew the critical meaning of Kimura's success or failure. Without help, the Japanese garrisons in New Guinea would never launch the glorious counteroffensive.

As the Allies prayed to their Christian God, so too did the Japanese petition their gods and honorable ancestors: "Let the wise and honorable Kimura bring this new infusion of life to Lae."

As the night wore on—1900, 2000, 2100, 2130—the supplications of the Japanese seemed more rewarding. One . . . two . . . three new flights of PBY's had scanned the sea along New Britain's northwest coast, from Kimbo Bay to Cape Gloucester; from New Britain to the Admiralties. However, they saw nothing; only the open stretches of the Bismarck Sea. By 2200, Kimura had made his 20 knots, sailed across the lower Bismarck Sea, and stolen into the coves of Kimbo Bay. At 2215 came the disappointed call to High Point. "This is Fly-by 4. Sorry, Mates, no sign of the Nip convoy."

And, incredibly, the ten P-38's of the 35th Fighter Group, because of the dense cover, had missed the convoy steaming right under their noses. The speedy Lightnings had scoured the area from Cape Gloucester Bay, where they saw only two sunken barges, to Huon Gulf. They had also searched the Dampier Strait and eastward to the Gazelle Peninsula. At 2330, the Lightnings did scour the Bismarck Sea along the coast of Kimbo Bay.

However, by the time the Lightnings got there, the "Eel of the Pacific" had settled his armada among the sheltered coves. Each ship lay snugly hidden behind a rock-ledged wall or a sloping ridge in an obscure lagoon. Above them, the restless, homeless nimbus clouds had finally touched the tallest of the *Shirayuki*'s masts. When the whine of P-38's echoed from the west, the Japanese soldiers and sailors had stiffened for a moment. But the sounds of aircraft soon disappeared to the south. The searchers had missed their quarry. And, five minutes later, came the final disappointing radio call from the P-38 search leader.

"Convoy lost. Repeat: convoy lost."

In the 90th Squadron communications tent, Larner and his crew reacted silently. Sal Dineo felt his body loosen. Subconsciously, he relished the possibility of missing the big pom-pom guns of destroyers and the booming explosions of 5-inch cruiser muzzles. But a guilt also crept into his mind and gnawed at his conscience. If he did not face the convoy—and destroy it—thousands of American and Australian troops might be destroyed.

Sergeant Joe Cardis merely bit his lips. Instead of sensing disappointment or relief, Cardis felt cheated. He was too young to recognize long-range danger. His mind felt only the emotional impact of the moment. The fears from today's mission to the Admiralties had already been replaced by the exciting thought of skip-bombing enemy ships. But now the inviting image of an exploding destroyer deck had faded with the disappointing radio message.

For Major Ed Larner, frustration rattled his nerves. His mind whirled, trying to re-expose the convoy through some kind of psychical power or mental telepathy. He had suffered too many months of defeat in the uneven Southwest Pacific conflict, and he could not accept the idea of missing the biggest battle of them all.

At Fifth Air Force headquarters in Port Moresby, the final, garbled radio message brought an emotional outburst from General Whitehead. "Goddam it! Goddam it!" he swore, pounding his fist on the desk. He tightened his lips, cutting deep crevices in his chin; and he glanced pleadingly, first at the huge map on the wall behind him and then at the two staff colonels standing before him.

But the officers said nothing. There was nothing to say.

Chapter Seven

A DEADLY GAME OF HIDE-AND-SEEK

The Southwest Pacific jungles display a most consistent nature. Never does the gnarled brush stop suffocating the young shoots that incessantly spring from the lush tropic soil. Never do the lizards stop devouring an overabundance of insects. Never do the swamps alter their stagnant surfaces of green and yellow scum. Never do the cascading mountain streams stop their foamy, tumbling roar. Like programmed robots, the dense trees meticulously rot the sunless brush under them, while the broiling sun mechanically scars the daily emergence of new kunai blades.

But as the jungle acts with certainty, the Southwest Pacific weather, in stark contrast, is the most unpredictable weather on earth. In minutes, angry winds from nowhere churn calm seas into maelstroms. In moments, tropic storm clouds cover a bright sky. Billowing cirrus and dense nimbus constantly challenge each other. And thunderheads, triggered by endless collisions of southern and northern air masses, erupt or vanish with the slightest rise or fall in the temperatures.

For all his talent and cunning, Admiral Masatomi Kimura gave little thought to these tropical whims. He was a strategist, a scientist and mathematician in the art of warfare. He was not a naturalist. Science had given accuracy to his pom-pom guns and his turret gun. Science had led him successfully through the maze of seas and islands. Science had helped him to overcome the hostile Southwest Pacific.

So at 2230 on the night of March 1, Kimura once more placed his faith in technology; this time in the meteorologists at Japan's main weather station in Rabaul. The admiral, sitting at a desk in his quarters, studied the memo his executive officer had brought him:

> Weather pattern quite stable. Nimbus formations building for past week over the Philippine and Yap tablelands. Content unusually high and dense, affecting entire Bismarck Archipelago. Pattern will continue for two more days; will ultimately dissipate over the New Guinea mountain tertiaries.

When Kimura finished, he dropped the sheet on his desk, rose from his chair and walked with Captain Tishayuna onto the bridge deck. In the past thirty minutes, there had been two heavy rain squalls and the deck was still wet. However, a soft breeze now whirled in comfortable wisps, pushing slight ripples across the lagoon in which the *Shirayuki* lay anchored. Kimura peered into the darkness at the misty outline of the *Arishio* that loomed like a silent black spectre. Then the admiral squinted behind him until he made out the bow of the transport nestled against a high cliff. Finally, he looked at the low overcast, the thick mists that still sped restlessly over the surface of the sea.

As he walked towards the forebridge, sailors on watch followed him with their eyes. They said nothing, not even to each other; but they wondered as did thousands of others waiting in this remote lagoon. How long would they stay here? When and where would they go? Cape Gloucester? Rooke Island? Madang? Gasmata? Perhaps even back to Rabaul?

After Kimura looked at his watch, he turned to Captain Tishayuna. "Captain, I would like the staff in my quarters within the half hour. Will you see to it, please?"

"Yes, Honorable Kimura."

The staff moved quickly. Within moments, small motor launches had carried Captains Miriou Genda and Kametaro Matsumoto to the *Shirayuki*. By 2300, piped aboard, they had joined Captain Tishayuna, Captain Yusi Watanabe, General Hatazo Adachi, General Sato Nakano, and Admiral Kimura in the chart room.

"Gentlemen," the admiral began, "we are here at 149.9, 5.4 in Kimbo Bay. At a maximum of ten knots we are much less than two days from Lae. Or within a few hours we can reach the shelter of Cape Gloucester or Rooke Island. And it appears it is difficult indeed to keep the Allied planes away from us. We could shelter ourselves at Cape Gloucester or. Rooke Island and from there move our cargos and passengers by barges to Finschafen; there to continue overland to Lae."

The subordinates said nothing.

"But many weeks might pass before our soldiers and equipment reach Lae," Kimura continued. "We ourselves understand that the American navy may soon gain respite from the Solomon campaign and their air force may soon be strengthened. The Honorable Adachi tells us that at *this* moment are the Allies weak in manpower and seapower and airpower. Thus, the Eighteenth Army needs reinforcements now if General Toru Okabe is to overrun Wau. And now is the time for General Adachi to begin his new offensive. To do these things the contents of this convoy must reach Lae immediately."

"Your words are accurately true, Admiral," General Adachi said.

"What are your thoughts, Admiral?" a staff member asked. "Do you suggest that we attempt to reach Lae, even though the Allies may strike with their bombers during the daylight hours?"

"Yes," Kimura answered. "We should sail at once."

"I would agree," General Adachi said.

"And I," General Nakano of the 51st Division added.

"But surely," the staff member said, placing his hand on the chart, "if the observation planes cannot be avoided, they will know when we come through the Dampier Strait and they will lash out at us as we cross the Solomon Sea."

Admiral Kimura now grinned, an unusual change to his sober face. "I have been assured by the meteorologists at Rabaul that this inclement weather will favor us for yet another two days. Even now the clouds hang so low they protect us even more than this dark lagoon. Did not American search planes, only a short time ago, fly within eyesight of us and fail to find us? They will have as much difficulty locating us even in the daylight hours. And, even if they do, what can they do in such inclement weather? They can only send inconsequential fighter planes or torpedo planes which will not harm us because our helmsmen have long ago learned to deal with them."

Once more, the staff held back on comment.

"And there is hope that their spy planes will not find us at all," Kimura continued. "They will no doubt resume their search in the morning, concluding that at such a time we will be sailing through the Dampier Strait. But they will not find us there, nor will they find us at Cape Gloucester since they do not know we are several hours behind schedule. They will come to one conclusion: we have hugged the coast and sailed for Gasmata—and shelter. But," he emphasized, "we will still be in the Bismarck Sea. Before the day is over, they will be forced to conclude we have returned to Rabaul or sailed to the Admiralties. By the day after tomorrow, before they can effectively search for us again, we shall be in Lae."

Impressed, the officers looked at each other and nodded.

"With the assurance that this heavy cloud cover will be with us for yet two days," Kimura continued, "I suggest we weigh anchor at once and sail for Lae at ten knots."

The staff officers discussed the move among themselves, and then General Adachi spoke. "The admiral speaks wisely. Surely there is not one among us who does not know how his cunning has many times foiled our enemy. And surely, we must not disappoint our troops who wait for us in Lae."

The other staff members nodded.

"Then let it be so," Admiral Kimura said. "Aweigh all vessels by 2400. Let the convoy be on a south by southeast course at one-six-zero."

And as the 22 vessels mustered in the murky darkness of Kimbo Bay, the morale of the Japanese sailors and soldiers was rejuvenated. They had felt uncertainties, anxieties, even frustrations. But all rallied as one with the admiral in his determination to reach Lae. They preferred, like their daring commander, the risk of disaster to the certainty of cowardice in the hidden coves of Kimbo Bay.

AT THE FIFTH AIR FORCE HEADQUARTERS in Port Moresby, a half hour before midnight, General Ennis Whitehead held a cup of coffee in his hand. He had enjoyed little rest for the past several hours, confining his supper to cups of hot black coffee. For three hours he had worked feverishly to ready his bomber and fighter groups to meet the obvious threat to New Guinea. For the following three hours, since the Reconn planes had been called off the search for the elusive convoy, Whitehead had been in a state of frustration, rattled over the loss of the armada and confused as to its probable location.

Colonel Pappy Gunn, together with the staff colonels, stood mutely in Whitehead's office. Aware of the general's dour mood, they would say nothing unless he gave them reason to. They only watched as the deputy commander sipped his coffee or ran his hand over the wall map.

"Right there," the general finally tapped a finger on the wall map. "They've got to be somewhere along the northwest coast of New Britain, heading for the Dampier Strait. They'll spend the whole night shooting across the Bismarck Sea. By morning they'll be passing Cape Gloucester and going into the Dampier Strait. They'll spend the day going through the strait with fighter escorts from Cape Gloucester and then start across the Solomon Sea tomorrow evening."

Thus it appeared that Kimura was correct. His delay of several hours in the coves of Kimbo Bay, putting him a hundred miles behind schedule, had deceived General Whitehead.

"Would they have doubled back to Rabaul?" a staff colonel asked.

Both the general and Pappy Gunn shook their heads. PBY's had covered the whole of the Bismarck Sea, even east of the Gazelle Peninsula. The Cats had then scoured the northern coast of New Britain. And only recently P-38's had blanketed the Dampier Strait and the entire northwest coast of New Britain, through Kimbo Bay to the Gazelle Peninsula. The Lightnings had even searched the Gazelle Peninsula. No, the convoy had not doubled back to Rabaul.

In fact, General Whitehead conceded, the convoy commander had thus far shown ingenious cunning. He had deliberately allowed the PBY's to track him openly during the daylight hours and then shot them out of the sky at dark to avoid further reconnaissance. Why? The Japanese admiral in charge of the convoy had a plan, a plan to thwart any Allied effort to find him. Whitehead nodded, mostly to himself. "The man in charge of that convoy knows what he's doing."

"Admiral Masatomi Kimura," one of the aides said quickly.

"Kimura?" Whitehead asked quizzically.

"The same man who got the Japanese convoy to Lae in January. The only Japanese admiral who could run convoys successfully on the Tokyo Express." When Whitehead frowned, the aide grinned. "New Britain intelligence, sir."

Whitehead nodded, then pursed his lips. The aide's comments had only strengthened his suspicions. This Admiral Kimura, Whitehead believed, had shown expert tactics as well as strong fortitude. He intended to outguess Fifth Air Force rather than fight them—and he had won the first round. No, Kimura had not retreated to Rabaul, but was on a full steam westward to be in the Dampier Strait by morning.

Whitehead again looked at the map behind him, and then ordered a fresh trio of PBY's to begin a new search along the western tip of New Britain at dawn. He also called for a reconnaissance search by speedy P-40's, unarmed and using auxiliary fuel tanks for greater range. The Warhawks should be across the Solomon Sea by dawn and begin a search through the Dampier Strait between the Bismarck and Solomon Seas. They should also search along the coastal areas of New Britain and Rooke Island.

When the general gave this new search order, he again looked at his map, tapping it once more—this time with the mess cup he held in his hand. "Yes, he'll be heading for the Dampier Strait by morning."

At midnight, General Whitehead finally called it a day. He retired on a small cot in his office, but he asked his staff to awaken him by 0500, or even sooner if anything new turned up. Meanwhile, Fifth Air Force personnel were to remain on duty throughout the night.

Also at midnight, the briefing had begun in earnest inside

the 43rd Bomb Group operations tent. The group commander had been outlining the bombing pattern for an hour.
"You might have to scramble for miles. By the time we get
there, those Jap ships will be scattered all over the sea."
Colonel Roger Ramey then turned to his 63rd Squadron commander. "I'll lead your squadron in. Then will come the 64th
Squadron. The 65th Squadron will come in last. All I can
say—each of you pick your target and go after it!"

Ramey studied his watch. "It's now 0100. Set your
watches." A moment later the colonel turned to the operations coordinator. "Are drivers and vehicles ready?"

"Yes, sir. The drivers are sacking out right in their jeeps.
They can move out to the strip on a minute's notice. And we
have the ground crews bunked right under their aircraft.
They'll have all ships preflighted by the time jeeps get our
flight crews out there."

"Good," the colonel said. Then he turned to the flyers.
"Any questions?" Silence. "Okay, that's it. Get a few hours'
sleep."

THE FIRST EVIDENCE OF DAYLIGHT, a band of eastern sky,
had brightened the horizon as a new flight of Aussie PBY's
roared along New Britain's northwest coast, above Cape
Gloucester. Meanwhile, a flight of six P-40's had already
droned into the Dampier Strait at the very break of dawn.
The Warhawks flew at 6,000 feet, above the clouds. When
they reached Rooke Island, the flight leader spoke into his
radio. "Okay boys, let's get under this cover and start looking."

The P-40's plunged into the clouds, dropped through the
overcast for several minutes, and then popped out of the mist
less than five hundred feet above the surface of the sea. They
spread out in a thirty-five-mile chain and cruised over the
Dampier Strait at 350 knots. They skimmed the sea north
along the New Britain coast to the Bismarck Sea and then
came east through the Dampier Strait along the coastal
waters of Rooke Island to the Solomon Sea. Then they flew
straight up the strait—all the way to Undoi Island.

When they had flown beyond Undoi Island, the flight
leader again called into his radio. "Okay boys, let's retrack to
the east. You wingmen, move east along the New Britain
coast, and you others search west along Rooke. I'm going to

take a look at Madang."

By 0515, the P-40 flight leader was over Madang. By now the day was bright, the area under him quite distinct. As he buzzed the harbor, the pilot noticed feverish activity. Japanese service troops were busily preparing jetties. Several barges were stationed in retrieve positions. The Japanese antiaircraft gunners only offered token flak as the P-40 circled over the bay. No interceptors rose to challenge. Perhaps the pilot had caught Madang off guard or perhaps the Japanese knew that interceptors would never catch the armorless P-40. Or, perhaps the sly Kimura wanted the P-40 reconnaissance plane to get a good look at the activity at Madang.

When the P-40 flight leader left Madang, he radioed Port Moresby. He told Fifth Air Force that he and his pilots had not seen a sign of the convoy in the Dampier Strait. They had scoured for miles on both sides and had even covered the northwest tip of New Britain. Further, they had seen no sign of the convoy around Rooke Island or as far west as Undoi Island.

The P-40 flight leader then reported that he himself had flown as far west as Madang without sign of the convoy. However, Madang, (about 200 miles up the coast from Lae) was in a state of feverish activity, readying docks, jetties, and barges. Japanese service troops seemed quite busy, as though they were preparing for company.

When this latest report reached General Whitehead, who had only slept lightly and intermittently through the night, he tried to decipher its meaning. Was it possible that Admiral Kimura's convoy was far to the north and heading for Madang instead risking a sail through the Dampier Strait into the Solomon Sea? He could make the voyage to Madang in relative safety, unload his troops and supplies, and then have them sent piecemeal from Madang to Lae via nighttime barges.

However Pappy Gunn was suspicious. From Australian infantry commanders, Gunn had learned much about the character of General Hatazo Adachi. The commander of the Eighteenth Army was a restless, impetuous man. Adachi had a glaring fault that was totally un-Japanese—he was impatient. If Adachi had convinced the Japanese Eighth Area staff in Rabaul to send a new division of troops to Lae, he would not settle for a dribble to come down from Madang over a period of weeks.

Gunn's reasoning held weight with Whitehead, and the general now ordered the PBY's to abandon their search between Gasmata and Cape Gloucester. Instead, they were to reconnoiter the Bismarck Sea between Undoi Island and the Gazelle Peninsula above the northwest coast of New Britain. Meanwhile, the P-40's were to continue a shuttle across the southwestern regions of the Bismarck Sea between the coast of New Britain and the coast of New Guinea. Both the P-40's and PBY's were to report any sightings immediately since the 43rd Bomb Group had been standing by in Port Moresby since 0500.

When Pappy Gunn and General Whitehead again studied the map of the Bismarck Archipelago, Whitehead slapped the back of his hand on the Dampier Strait. "I don't understand it. They have to be in that strait or somewhere near it." He turned to the radio operator. "Tell that P-40 flight leader to leave a couple of search planes combing the Dampier Strait."

"Yes sir," the radioman answered.

Now, as Pappy Gunn and General Whitehead took another coffee break, Gunn looked at the map with a heavy frown. He fell into such deep meditation that he drew a quizzical look from General Whitehead.

"What's the matter?"

"I know it sounds crazy," Gunn said, "but maybe that convoy is still a long way from the Dampier Strait. Maybe they waited 'til dark to chase off the reconnaissance PBY's so they could change course during the nighttime hours with little chance of exposure. Suppose they pulled into some of those obscure coves around Kimbo Bay or the Gazelle Peninsula and waited for a chance to make a run for the Dampier Strait? That would be a good reason why reconnaissance couldn't find them last night or this morning."

Whitehead stroked his chin. The PBY's and P-38's had covered the sea lanes all the way to the Gazelle Peninsula. They would have certainly spotted them around Kimbo Bay or the Peninsula. But Gunn disagreed. He reminded the general that the search had taken place at night and that the overcast had been so thick it practically touched the sea. They couldn't have found a thing last night, especially if that convoy had hidden itself in a cove along New Britain's northwest coast. Gunn then suggested they search the huge Kimbo Bay area from the Dampier Strait eastward.

Whitehead agreed and turned to the radio operator. "Send a couple of those PBY's and a few of those P-40's to the east to search the Kimbo Bay waters—all the way to the Gazelle Peninsula. I want some of those reconns tracking along the coast and others farther out to sea."

WHEN THIS LATEST REQUEST TO SCOUR Kimbo Bay reached the P-40 search leader, he frowned in disbelief. The convoy had left Rabaul 30 hours ago. Even at seven to nine knots, the armada had to be well beyond Kimbo Bay. Besides, no reconn plane had seen those Japanese ships in that area last night. It would be a waste of time.

"Just do it," the heavy voice of High Point said.

"Okay. Out!" the P-40 flight leader said.

Meanwhile, aboard the *Shirayuki*, Admiral Kimura stood on the bridge. The morning was cooler and less humid than the night before, especially on the open sea. Kimura took a deep breath and sauntered to the forebridge in a pre-breakfast stroll. He scanned the convoy around him, watching the complement of ships ply heavily through the choppy, open sea.

"What is our heading?" Kimura asked his executive officer.

"148.1 east, 5.8 degrees south," Captain Tishayuna answered. We are now 80 knots east of Undoi Island. Speed is still at ten knots; course remains at one-six-zero."

"Good," Kimura nodded. "Maintain present speed and course."

The admiral looked at his watch: 0530 hours. He pursed his lips and stared gratefully at the heavy cloud cover above him. He nearly smiled, but his dark eyes suddenly widened as he peered into the growing daylight. A tint of white paled his face. A patch of blue sky loomed on the horizon. Quickly he pivoted and peered anxiously to the south. Again his eyes widened. Cracks appeared in the thick cloud cover. The dark mists were dissipating before new white masses. Billowy cirrus clouds were shoving aside the gray cloud cover.

Nature was showing contempt for Kimura and the science of meteorology.

"Captain! Captain Tishayuna!" the admiral shouted.

"Yes, Admiral." The executive officer quickly strode forward.

"Does my sight falter?" Kimura asked anxiously. "Do I sincerely see this horrible disappointment in the sky? The clouds," he pointed. "Do they not disjoin? Or does the strain of this most important voyage play tricks on my eyes?"

Captain Tishayuna scanned the skies and his mouth flew open. "Your eyes do not deceive you, Admiral. The cloud cover indeed ruptures."

"And where are we? Where are we?"

"Eighty knots from Undoi Island," Captain Tishayuna said. "Well into the open sea."

Now the patch of sky to the southeast had cleansed the heavens of clouds. The entire horizon was a wide field of azure blue. To the flanks, patches of blue had emerged through the broken masses of overhead nimbus formations.

"Alert all gunners, Captain!" Kimura said urgently. "Bring closer to the convoy our Mitsubishi I escorts from Cape Gloucester."

"Yes, Admiral."

"And pray that our honorable ancestors will favor us in this crisis."

While three of the P-40's continued to search the sea lanes between New Britain and New Guinea, the first wave of P-40's was heading up the Vitiaz Strait, searching as far as Undoi Island. The cloud cover was breaking up and a bright sun exploded flashes of sunlight on the Warhawks' plexiglass cockpits. It was during these flights that the call came from Port Moresby to search in the Kimbo Bay area.

"We're going straight east," the P-40 flight leader told his patrol. "We've got a revised request to search across Kimbo Bay all the way from the Dampier Strait to the Gazelle Peninsula."

"Are you kidding?! Why?" one of the pilots scowled.

"Because High Point says so."

The three P-40 reconnaissance planes now turned eastward. Then at 0600 hours, cruising comfortably at 300 knots and 3,000 feet, and fifty knots beyond Cape Gloucester, the Americans flew into a swarm of Zeros. The fighters, streaking across the sky from two o'clock, were apparently responding to Admiral Kimura's orders.

"Jesus H. Christ, look at that!" one of the pilots blurted into his mouthpiece. "Where in hell are they coming from?"

"Cape Gloucester would be my guess," the flight leader replied. "But we're not hanging around to find out. High Point can go to hell."

The flight leader ordered a 90-degree turn, north. The three Warhawks zoomed forward at full speed, 400 knots, deep into the Bismarck Sea. The Zeros gave chase but the reconn planes, armorless and light, easily outran them. The P-40's had not flown ten minutes, however, when, with startling suddenness, they zoomed over their quarry. At first the sea exposed hazy globs of dark shapes. But seconds later, Kimura's convoy, spread out in the *hochi* pattern, loomed large and clear.

Stunned, one of the pilots mechanically switched on his radio: "Holy Christ! Holy Christ!"

"This is High Point, High Point!" the heavy voice from Port Moresby rasped. "What the hell are you yelling about?"

"The convoy, High Point, the convoy!" the awestricken pilot answered. He had regained enough of his composure to check his instruments. "Bearing 149.2 east, 5.4 degrees south. Moving at about ten knots. Course: about one-six-zero."

"What?!" The heavy voice was now astonished. "Repeat, repeat!"

"You heard us," the search leader chimed in. "Bearing 149.2 east, 5.4 degrees south. They're wide open in the middle of the Bismarck Sea. Bring on your heavies, there's nothing but pure blue up here. And be sure to send fighters along. By the time the show starts, the whole damn area's gonna be full of Zekes!"

General Whitehead peered at his map, almost touching it with his nose. "About 148, right in the middle of the Bismarck!" he cried, barely containing his elation. "Goddam it, Pappy, you were right! Kimura did hole up around Kimbo Bay." A wide grin cracked the general's face. "We got 'em, Pappy, we got 'em!"

"They won't be able to reach any cover for at least three hours," Gunn said. "And the 43rd is already moving out. They'll pick up their fighter escort off the coast of Gona."

The two men stopped and listened to the strain of heavy engines coming from the area of Eight-Mile Drome. Whitehead checked his watch and smiled. 0605. Only an hour late. By 0800 the Flying Forts would be over the convoy. Whitehead turned and looked at the huge map of the Bismarck Archipelago. He slapped the chart several times with the back of his hand. He had hoped to catch Kimura at Cape Gloucester or Rooke Island where his air units could at least do partial damage before the ships could find shelter and protection from Japanese interceptors and antiaircraft guns.

But never in his wildest dreams had Whitehead ever thought he'd be lucky enough to catch the convoy totally exposed, right smack dab in the middle of the Bismarck Sea!

Chapter Eight

BATTLE OF THE BISMARCK SEA: ROUND 1

At the end of World War II, several high-ranking Japanese commanders admitted that because of more than expected resistance, their timetable for conquering the Western Pacific had been seriously delayed. These delays came in the Philippines, Java, and New Guinea. By the time Japan was prepared to invade Australia, the Allies had grown too strong for such a thrust. A multitude of factors caused this delay: stubbornness from retreating ground troops, well-trained Allied airmen, stings by brazen Allied naval units, scorched-earth policies, and overextended supply lines.

But, if one single factor more than anything else slowed the Japanese juggernaut in the Western Pacific, it was the B-17 Flying Fortress. The Japanese fighter far outclassed the earlier American P-39 and P-40 fighter planes, but the Zeros found the Flying Fortress to be exactly that—an aerial fortress that was extremely difficult to shoot out of the air.

Before the war started, Japanese intelligence had learned much about the Flying Fortress, and they did not like what they learned. The long-range, heavy bomber might prove to be a real threat to their plans. So when war broke out on December 7, 1941, the first target of the Japanese high command was the 19th Heavy Bomb Group's B-17's at Clark Field in the Philippines and the 22nd Bomb Group's B-17's at Hickam Field in Hawaii.

Two squadrons, twenty-two Flying Forts, were housed at Clark Field. Fortunately, most of them had been airborne at the time of the December 8 noonday attack on Clark by Japanese bombers. The 19th Bomb Group had thus lost only a half dozen of their B-17's. The others of the group had been on the way to the American base of Delmonte on Mindanao. At Hawaii, none of the 22nd Bomb Group's B-17's were on the ground during the December 7th surprise attack. They had been on flight maneuvers and so escaped the Pearl Harbor holocaust.

Because the B-17's could operate out of Delmonte and do considerable damage to enemy operations, the Japanese conquest of the Philippines stretched out to May, 1942, long beyond their timetable. Besides shipping and dock facilities on both Luzon and Mindanao, the B-17's often destroyed troop concentrations, tank columns, and airfields to further upset the Japanese schedule. The long-range Forts had often evacuated hordes of key military personnel before the Japanese could kill or capture them. And finally, the B-17's had successfully reconnoitered Japanese movements throughout the Western Pacific to help General MacArthur withdraw his forces with minimum losses.

Swarms of Zeros had always jumped the unescorted B-17's (there was little fighter protection available early in the war). But despite dozens of hits, the Zeros rarely knocked one of the big birds out of the air, and often lost fighters to B-17 gunners.

Later, B-17's based at Darwin in northern Australia harrassed the Japanese convoys and ground operations in Java. And when it became obvious that Java was doomed, the B-17's evacuated most of the military personnel to Australia. Enraged, the Japanese sent a hundred bombers to Darwin to wipe the B-17's off the face of the earth. But the B-17's were airborne at the time and escaped the raid to fight another day. The frustrated Japanese found themselves so busy dealing with the tough-skinned B-17, they had to delay the invasion of Darwin—an invasion that never came off.

Then the overworked, badly worn Fortresses, amazingly durable, destroyed docks, runways, repair shops, troopships, and other logistical targets in New Guinea to further thwart the Japanese.

And in the Coral Sea battle, many experts believe that a fear of attacks by B-17's, now based in Townsville, Australia, prompted the Japanese to withdraw the invasion fleet heading for Port Moresby. They were not sure they could hold Moresby against B-17 attacks.

In early 1943, Colonel Roger Ramey, a squadron leader of the old 19th Bomb Group, and now commander of the 43rd Bomb Group, said this: "Our planes were tired, worn out, and abused beyond limits. We had thrown caution to the wind. We took off and landed on short landing fields, we ignored wind directions, and our gunners took on whole squadrons of Zero interceptors. Still, we could almost always bring the Fort home—just so long as one of its four engines was still operating."

Ramey vividly recalled the Zero attack on Captain Kelly's B-17. Kelly had been making a reconnaissance flight in his lone Flying Fortress over Luzon in January, 1942. A squadron of Zeros had jumped him. They had destroyed the B-17 instrument panel, blown away the top turret and its gunner, punctured the oxygen tank, ignited the left wing, set aflame the bomb bay, cut the elevator cables, and riddled the wings and fuselage until the plane looked like a piece of flying junk. But Kelly brought the shattered bomber safely home.

The ruggedly built B-17 had indeed been a thorn in the side of the Japanese. Zero pilots had marvelled at the Fort's ability to take punishment.

Was it any wonder then that General Whitehead decided to send in first his B-17's when reconnaissance planes again found the Lae Resupply Convoy in the Bismarck Sea? And nothing could have delighted more the commander of the 43rd Bomb Group, Colonel Roger Ramey. He hoped to administer a fatal blow to the Japanese in retaliation for the suffering and humiliation he and his overworked B-17 crews had experienced since the beginning of the war. Ramey hoped that the Japanese would find in the Bismarck Sea not a B-17 thorn in their side this time, but a fatal dagger.

BY 0630 ON THE MORNING OF 2 MARCH 1943, the twenty-eight B-17's of the 43rd Bomb Group had reached the Solomon Sea. They had settled into a parade of seven four-plane diamonds at 10,000 feet as they rumbled northwards towards the Bismarck Sea. The bombers looked motionless except for the props that whirled like cellophane circles. The big 1200-HP engines hummed like deafening dynamos.

Two thousand feet above the B-17's only the ridged slabs of white cirrus clouds and the darting shapes of P-38's marred the blue sky. The Lightnings of the 35th and 49th Fighter Groups were under the command of Colonel Bob Morrissey, a veteran pilot who had escorted B-17's for nearly a year, beginning as a P-40 pilot in Darwin, Australia.

The bulk of the Lightnings frolicked above the big bombers in lazy arches or curling swoops. Only one flight had moved ahead of the formation, searching for the prey like hungry falcons.

For more than an hour the heavily laden bombers had droned northwestward from Port Moresby; first over the Owen Stanley Range of Papua, and now over the Solomon Sea. The sun had fully risen from the east and the last orange hues of dawn had faded into a pale blue sky. Within the bombers, pilots and copilots tempered the monotonous flight with repetitious checking and rechecking of instruments. Gunners repeatedly whirled in their gunseats or swiveled the big twin fifties that jutted from the Flying Fort fuselages. Bombardiers checked sights, navigators checked charts, and radiomen worked on equipment. And all kept a watchful eye for enemy aircraft.

Less than a hundred miles northwest, Kimura's convoy also waited. Japanese gunners sat warily in their pom-pom pits or 5-inch turret gun stations. Sick bay corpsmen prepared tables, medicines, or bandages for the casualties sure to come. Armament crews stacked the 3-inch and 5-inch shells that would feed the ack-ack barrels. And besides the gunnery and armament crews, only battle directing signalmen and officers moved about the exposed decks of the ships. The ships' service crews remained in sheltered areas. The 15,000 troops, fitted with helmets and life preservers, had been herded into the holds.

Admiral Kimura made no attempt to increase the convoy's ten-knot pace. He wanted no speed up to create a futile strain on the engines. Nor had he altered the checkerboard *hochi* pattern except to spread the vessels to 1500 yards. The increased gaps would allow individual ships better maneuvering room without endangering companion vessels.

High above the plodding convoy, fifty Zeros swarmed in three- to six-thousand-foot heights, hovering like homeless wasps. But while most of the aircraft were stationed over the armada, a few of the Japanese fighter planes had vaulted outward to reconnoiter the east in a 180-degree radius.

Although a couple hundred fighter planes were based on the land masses off the Bismarck Sea and Dampier Strait, not all of them were committed to battle, a strategy that would have an important impact on the military action. The Zeros over the convoy now would only loiter for two hours in the open skies before a second group of fighters would relieve them and continue the vigil over the convoy. The Japanese took the attitude that if needed, they could quickly dispatch necessary reserve aircraft into battle.

At precisely 0800, the first white dots blipped on the radar screen of the picket destroyer *Asashio*, the flag of the convoy's destroyer division. The two operators straightened in their seats and made their report: 15,000 yards off starboard; bearing one-nine-zero.

Captain Mirouru Genda, commander of the destroyer division, raced to the foredeck of the destroyer, his executive officer and gunnery chief after him. All three *Asashio* officers raised their field glasses and scanned the southeastern skies. Soon they saw the misty dots on the horizon, like a vanguard of a locust invasion that every decade or so destroyed the wheat fields of Kyushu.

Captain Genda ordered all destroyers on alert; gunners especially were to prepare for enemy approach at the bearing of one-nine-zero. Genda then notified Admiral Kimura.

Within moments, whoop alarms sounded on ship after ship within the convoy. The wails echoed in grating rasps, and in the holds of the transports the Japanese combat soldiers stiffened. In the supply rooms, magazine compartments, radio areas, and other parts of the vessels, naval personnel scampered to their posts. On the decks of the cruisers and destroyers the gun-crews hastily readied their pom-pom and turret antiaircraft guns, while armament crews hurried about the decks with ammunition. Overhead, the Zeros jelled into a formation of squares and arched in unison to meet the ominous swarm of approaching black dots.

"Jolly Leader, Jolly Leader," Colonel Bob Morrissey radioed Colonel Ramey of the 43rd Bomb Group, "convoy ahead. They've broken formation and they're scooting around the sea like water bugs."

The Fifth Air Force airmen had found the convoy in the Bismarck Sea north of Cape Gloucester.

"We're going upstairs to hit their cover," Morrissey radioed Ramey.

"We read you. Roger and out," Ramey answered calmly.

As the big B-17 bombers bored into the convoy, the Lightnings, at about 400 knots, waded into the defending Zeros in an aerial cavalry charge. Suddenly the opposing planes clashed in exploding bits of swerving, twisting shapes. The whine of aircraft echoed across the sky. The staccato of fifty calibers rattled to the horizons. Dying aircraft sliced through the sky or fell towards the sea, trailing white or black smoke. For the moment, at least, the Zeros could not reach the bombers below.

MEANWHILE, RAMEY'S TIGHT FORMATIONS of B-17's dropped like descending balloons until they settled at 5,000 feet above the surface of the sea. The four-plane diamonds came within 2,000 yards of the convoy when antiaircraft fire rumbled across the sea. As fast as Japanese gunners ejected empty casings, armament crews replenished the expended ammo.

When the B-17's droned into the scattered convoy and unleashed their cargos of thousand-pound bombs, the surface vessels cut erratic wakes as they maneuvered to escape the aerial attack. The first diamond of planes had only splashed the sea water in white explosions, missing completely their destroyer target.

Admiral Kimura calmly watched the initial assault. The veteran of the Tokyo Express had long ago learned to cope with descending bombs from high-altitude aircraft. As expected, the next diamond sought out his cruisers as bombers always sought out a convoy's sentinel warships. The admiral stood alertly on the bridge of the *Shirayuki*. As the quadrangle of approaching B-17's bomb bays opened, Kimura shouted to the cruiser's wheel officer. "Ready port!"

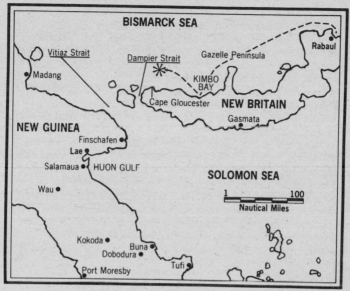

Map 4: Flying Fortresses attack convoy in open Bismarck Sea.

Then, as the bombs dropped from the bellies of the Forts, he cried again: "Hard to port! Fully forty-five degrees."

Kimura braced himself against the railing as the helmsman spun the big cruiser to the left. The engines strained and the heavy black smoke spiraled from the cruiser's stacks. The port prow scooped up a patch of sea in exploding foam — like the sudden release of a capped geyser. But, the big warship had barely turned-to when Kimura cried again. "To starboard! Starboard, full forty-five degrees."

Again the ship slapped through the heavy seas. Now the starboard aft sent out the exploding foams of sea water. Within seconds the stern of the cruiser had skidded to port and straightened. The foaming wash from the zig-zagging turns still boiled when a dozen or more thousand-pound bombs slammed into the sea fifty to a hundred yards off the cruiser's starboard hull. The explosions jolted the *Shirayuki* along with men and equipment. Huge crests of water slammed against the hull and washed over the decks. But the

Shirayuki and her crew escaped unharmed.

Nor did the *Shirayuki's* sailors freeze. Both stern and starboard gunners continued to throw pom-pom shells at the passing diamonds of B-17's. The *Shirayuki* had escaped the rain of bombs, but not all of the Flying Fortresses escaped the gauntlet of exploding flak. One burst tore open the left side of a B-17; another burst ripped open the left side of its tail. The big American bomber dropped momentarily, but then straightened and remained airborne.

Other vessels in the convoy were not so fortunate. One of the 7,000-ton transports became the first victim of Operation Bismarck Sea. The commander, cautiously directing strategy from the bridge of his ship, watched two B-17's soar towards his port side. He waited until the bombs had left the bomb bays and then ordered a hard turn to starboard. The transport had escaped the bulk of exploding bombs, but one of the thousand pounders struck the aft of the ship and chopped out a piece of the stern, including the rudder.

Now the wounded transport plied in a dizzy, uncontrollable gait. A third B-17 wasted no time. The pilot brought the big bomber to a dangerous 3,000 feet, despite the rattle of 5-inch guns. The Flying Fortress came within a thousand yards of the ship before the pilot ordered the bombardier to release four one-thousand-pound bombs. After the bombs left the bomb bay, the pilot veered the big Fort upwards like an overgrown fighter plane.

The desperate helmsman could not manuever the ship and bombs raked the wounded vessel from stern to bow. The first explosion opened the stern; the second tore apart the bridge and its staff, including the commander; the third detached the smoke stacks; and the fourth hit the ack-ack magazine storage area. The vessel fell apart in a series of disintegrating explosions. When the concussions ended, the ship was enveloped in smoke and fire, listing fatally to starboard. With no time for lifeboats for rafts, those aboard who survived the holocaust scrambled over the sides and plopped into the sea.

The destroyer *Asagumo* wheeled to port and steamed quickly through the rippling waters for rescue operations. By the time the warship reached the bedlam, the transport was settling to the bottom of the Bismarck Sea.

Colonel Ramey, from his own B-17, nodded in satisfaction

Official U.S. Air Force Photo

A troop transport is bombed during Bismarck Sea battle. Note spray from near-miss on far side amidship.

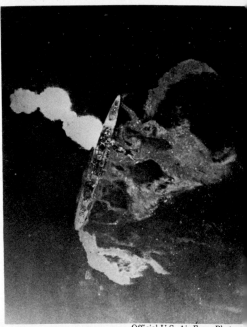

A-20 of the 89th Bomb Group zooms away from freighter after dropping its 500-pound bombs at mast height. To the right, a destroyer spews oil slicks after being stopped dead in the water by bomb hits.

Official U.S. Air Force Photo

Official U.S. Air Force Photo

Allied plane zooms in at mast height, right over smokestack of speeding destroyer. Note Japanese sailors taking cover.

A pair of 3rd Group skip bombers close in on freighter in Huon Gulf (*above*). On right, a freighter burns after high altitude attack by B-17's on the afternoon of March 2, 1943.

Official U.S. Air Force Photo

All that remains of Japanese barges which were burned or sunk
by Allied planes on a strafing run along the New Guinea coast.

Official U.S. Air Force Photo

Official U.S. Air Force Photo

Pictured *above* **is quartet of U.S. fighter pilots who shot down enemy aircraft during dogfights over Wau: (l to r) Lt. Eugene C. De Boer of Hammond, Ind.; Lt. Lewis D. Rainer of Louisville, Ga.; Capt. Thomas H. Winburn of San Antonio, Texas; and Lt. Henry L. Campbell of Ruston, La. P-38 Lightnings** *(bottom)* **are lined up on Papua.**

Official U.S. Air Force Photo

Official U.S. Air Force Photo

Crew members of the "Strawberry Roan," an A-20, pose in front of their aircraft: (l to r) Lt. Jarrett B. Roan of Shreveport, La.; unidentified airman; Sgt. Thomas Clark; Pvt. Ascension M. Mata of Fort Worth, Texas; and Sgt. William M. Sherman of Hague, N.Y. *Bottom,* **a Beaufighter, one of the major aircraft used by the Australian air force.**

Official U.S. Air Force Photo

Official U.S. Air Force Photo

Papuan natives prove invaluable in action against Japanese. Below, men are shown refueling Lockheed P-38 on Feb. 28, 1943.

at this first kill. The colonel had barely grinned, however, when two Zeros whirred out of the sky and dove at the wing position bomber. The B-17 gunners opened up with a barrage of twin fifties, the chatter vibrating through the fuselage. But the swooping Zeros successfully escaped the stream of fire while they themselves ripped several tracer shots through the fuselage and sheered off the aileron of the bomber's tail.

As the Zeros peeled away, the B-17 strained upwards, trying to right itself despite its damaged tail. However, the gunners of the *Asagumo* loosened a barrage of accurate ack-ack, even as the destroyer plucked survivors from the sea. The 5-inch flak bursts shattered the B-17's belly and ignited the gas tanks. The Flying Fort exploded in midair and plopped into the sea in a stream of flame.

Other B-17's not as harassed, continued to fly over the zig-zagging vessels and dumped their thousand pounders. But the Forts sank no more vessels although they did effect considerable damage.

One bomber hit a transport's starboard gunwale, killing a dozen Japanese soldiers and slowing down the vessel. A second swarm of bombers scored with thousand pounders on the forecastle of the 10,000-ton *Nojima Maru*, ripping out a quarter of her deck. Dozens of crammed 77th Brigade soldiers died in the holds along with several of the transport's sailors. Another bomb, a near miss, clawed the starboard gunwale and knocked out the kitchen and mess area.

Two other diamonds, attacking the convoy from the port quarter, heavily damaged two destroyers while using a spread-out saturation pattern. Twenty-two bombs rained down. The gyrating twists and turns of the sleek tin cans could not completely foil the attack. The fore turrets and a stack of one destroyer disappeared in an eruption of metallic fragments, while the foredeck suffered a huge gap from a third hit. The destroyer twisted and rolled like a wounded whale, but she remained afloat under her own power.

The second destroyer managed to swerve hard to port to escape most of the descending bombs, but her stern almost disappeared. Chunks of metal scattered and plopped into the sea, causing a hundred-yard radius of foaming sea. However, this destroyer, too, remained afloat.

Finally, the B-17's had slightly damaged one of the freighters with a pair of near misses.

Thus, while 28 heavy bombers had unleased over 50 tons of bombs, they had sunk but one ship—proof that the Japanese had become adept at warding off high-altitude aerial strikes. And this despite the fact that the P-38's had successfuly warded off most of the Zero attempts to harass the bomber assault.

"White Leader, this is Jolly Leader!" Colonel Ramey called Colonel Morrissey. "Our run's completed. Let's go home."

"Roger," Morrissey answered.

AS THE FORMATIONS OF BOMBERS and escorting P-38's veered westward, Admiral Kimura surveyed his damage from the heavy bomb attack. The transport *Kyoikusei Maru* was lost, but the destroyer *Asagumo* was picking up many survivors. Another *maru* transport and two destroyers had been damaged, one seriously. A freighter was slightly damaged with no loss of life. In casualties, they could count 63 dead and 174 wounded. The Japanese had also lost four Zeros.

As to American aircraft, the Japanese had downed one of the B-17's and seriously damaged another. There was no loss to the American P-38 escort squadrons. Thus, the first round in Operation Bismarck Sea went to the Fifth Air Force.

"Keep gunners alert," Kimura told his staff, "and revert to course one-six-zero at ten knots. *Asagumo* may join us when she has completed her rescue operations."

Kimura then straightened and leaned against the bridge railing of his flagship. Though disturbed by the transport loss and the damage to other ships, he felt a consolation. The Americans had thrown the bulk of their heavy bombers against him on this first strike, but the convoy had suffered only minimal damage.

But Kimura could not rest easy, for radar had again picked up enemy aircraft at the one-nine-zero bearing. This time the B-24's of the 321st Group were out to attack the Lae Resupply Convoy. By 0800 the Liberators had been well on their way, escorted by an undermanned squadron of twelve P-40's that carried wing auxiliary fuel tanks. However, the B-24 group could offer only nine serviceable planes for this morning's sortie and three of these had been forced to abort because of varied engine, electrical, or other problems. So, only six of the B-24's would reach the target.

Kimura ordered his staff to alert all helmsmen for quick maneuvers for this second high-altitude bomb attack. Then, the convoy commander scanned the southeastern skies with his field glasses. But he could not see any sign of the enemy. Thick wads of cirrus clouds had reappeared on the horizon.

The broken cloud formations were again closing quickly and thickly over the Bismarck Sea, and the Liberators experienced severe difficulty. They found few opportunities to make a systematic attack on the scattered convoy because they could find few breaks in the clouds to make bomb drops. Further, two squadrons of Zero fighters had successfully neutralized the effectiveness of the twelve P-40 escorts and the Zeros were able to harass the six Liberators during the entire bombing raid. The B-24's found little time for an attack, especially at 10,000 feet. The fleeting moments over the convoy ended with only some minor hits and near misses.

The 321st returned to Port Moresby in disappointment. They didn't mind the Zero harassment; they had expected as much. But they did not have the open skies as did the 43rd Group before them. However, they did have a consolation: they had not lost any bombers and none of the badly outnumbered P-40's had been lost, while, astonishingly, they had claimed two Zero kills.

Pappy Gunn and General Whitehead now agreed that further attacks with the heavy cloud cover would be useless. Only medium bombers might do the job now, and Whitehead decided to wait until the convoy reached Cape Gloucester, within medium bomber range. That would be about mid-afternoon on this second day of March. He would send in first the B-25's of the 38th Group and then the B-25's and A-20's of the 3rd Bomb Group.

By 1500 on the afternoon of 2 March, the twelve B-25's of the 38th Group, under Colonel Fay Upthegarde, had cleared the Dampier Strait and sighted their objective convoy about 50 knots northwest of Cape Gloucester.

Back at Dobodura, ground crews had been pre-flighting the B-25's and A-20's of the 3rd Bomb Group. Flight crews were already on the airstrip. They would take off as soon as the P-38's of the 49th and 35th Fighter Groups had been reloaded and refueled to escort the 3rd Group on the bomb run to destroy Kimura's slow-moving convoy.

Meanwhile, inside the 90th Squadron radio tent, Major Ed Larner and several other pilots listened eagerly to the radio reports from the returning B-17 bombers. The 43rd Group airmen had confirmed the sinking of a transport and the possible sinking of a second transport. The pilots of the 90th frowned in disappointment at the low score from the heavy bombers, but then a new voice suddenly came over the radio.

"This is 30 Leader, 30 Leader," the voice of Colonel Upthegarde came over the radio band. "Target at one o'clock; 10,000 yards. Get ready to scramble."

"We'll look for bandits," the commander of the escorting 35th Fighter Group answered. The Group's P-39's, along with attached Australian Beaufighters, were escorting the 38th Bomb Group. These were the only fighter planes available. The fighter commander then ordered his fighter pilots to drop their auxiliary fuel tanks and move out to search for any Japanese fighters who might be guarding the convoy.

Again Colonel Upthegarde's voice came over the 90th Squadron radio. "Flak at 3,000 yards. Pick your targets and scramble in one minute." The 38th Group commander then scolded High Point in Port Moresby. "I thought you said it was clear out here? Nimbus clouds are moving in all over the place."

Fickle Mother Nature had been at it again. She had first cleared and then covered the skies over the Bismarck Sea this morning. Then, later in the day, she had cleared the skies again. Now, as the 38th Group's B-25's approached the target, Mother Nature was again closing in the Bismarck Sea with dense clouds.

When Colonel Upthegarde complained of the weather, Major Ed Larner frowned and stepped outside the 90th Squadron radio shack to scan the skies. Erratic clouds, some a thick white and others a thick gray, were drifting swiftly overhead. The sun had vanished under one of the unusually heavy formations. The 90th Squadron commander lit a cigarette, leaned against the tent, and tried to relax. However, a few moments later, one of the pilots burst out of the ready tent and shook Larner.

"They got a cruiser! Fay's boys got a cruiser!"

Larner rushed back inside the radio shack where other

pilots were huddled closely to the radio, listening in deep anticipation. Besides the claimed sinking of a cruiser, 38th Group pilots had also claimed other hits: three hits on a freighter which was now listing to port; fatal hits on one of the tankers that had left the tanker enveloped in heavy smoke and sinking rapidly; hits on a second tanker that had left the ship rudderless.

Larner bit his lips and cursed under his breath. There wouldn't be a goddam thing left by the time 3rd Group got there.

FINALLY, AT 1530, A NON-COM POPPED his head into the 90th Squadron radio shack. "The fighters are reloaded and ready to go."

The pilots scrambled out of the radio shack and hurried to their waiting Mitchells. The B-25's and A-20's of the 3rd Group were sitting on the taxi strips, rocking back and forth like anxious greyhounds. Their whining props, straining to pull the planes free of the wheel chucks, whirled up dust clouds that ran the length of the taxi dispersal areas.

Other flight crews of the 3rd Bomb Group had emerged from a dozen different nooks and crannies to hurry towards their aircraft. Some came in jeeps or command cars; others scurried out of tents, or from revetment areas, or from under tree overhangs, or even from the control tower. Within minutes the three-man B-25 crews and two-man A-20 crews hoisted themselves into their poised aircraft.

As Ed Larner settled into his cockpit he looked out of the port window and addressed his crew chief. "Anything more from the 38th?"

"They definitely got the cruiser and tanker," the sergeant said, "and they damaged some of the ships. Zekes shot down a couple of the P-40 escorts."

Larner nodded and closed the port window.

The major checked with Sal Dineo and Joe Cardis, then sat patiently in his B-25 for several minutes while the A-20's, in pairs, zoomed down the Dobodura bomber strip and rose upwards into the sky. And not until the last A-20 of the 89th Squadron had shot skyward, did Larner push the throttle of his Mitchell while the crew chief yanked away the wheel chucks. The B-25 jerked forward, spun to the left, and taxied up to the end of the dispersal area. As he took off from

Dobodura, the other B-25's of the 90th Squadron followed. Then the six B-25's of the 13th Squadron followed the 90th.

As the mixed B-25 and A-20 aircraft droned out to the Solomon Sea, the twin-fuselaged P38's streaked out to meet them.

"We're with you, Alpine Leader," came the voice of Colonel Bob Morrissey who was leading the combined 49th and 35th Fighter Groups. The Lightning pilots had already been out this morning with B-17's and they were now escorting the 3rd Bomb Group.

For nearly an hour the planes droned northwestward uneventfully. In Larner's B-25, copilot Sal Dineo had at least momentarily allayed his fear with an anxious desire to attack the Japanese convoy. From the cramped seat of his turret bubble, Joe Cardis yawned, tired of looking at the parade of B-25's behind his own squadron lead plane. Occasionally, Cardis looked down at the wide expanse of Solomon Sea or he stared above him. The patches of blue sky were disappearing rapidly as clouds converged from several different directions.

Cardis shrugged and looked down to check his ammo supply. He checked his guns, swiveling them, cocking the breech, fingering the triggers. When he next looked into the sky, ten minutes later, the last patch of blue had disappeared. Overhead were only thick globs of white and they were rapidly turning gray.

Cardis spun in an 180-degree arc and looked to the fore. The same nimbus clouds extended as far as he could see. He frowned. Foggy mists were drifting silently past his plexiglass-enclosed turret. The sergeant picked up his intercom radio. "Major, we're moving through some awfully heavy clouds."

"I don't know what's happening, Sergeant," Larner said, "we're at 5,000 feet and the stuff is getting worse."

During the next five minutes the fog wisped past the turret more frequently. It became thicker, denser. Soon the vapor masses had joined and become a heavy mist around the aircraft. By now Cardis could only see shadowy outlines of the 13th Squadron behind him.

In the cabin, Major Larner and Lt. Dineo also squinted. The tail flight of the 89th Squadron's A-20's in front of them were only hazy shapes. Nowhere could the two airmen detect the escorting Lightnings. The very sky had become one overpowering nimbus mass, blinding them. The sun had vanished as had the sea below them. The entire formation was buried in an endless mist.

Larner looked at his instrument panel: still at 5.0, and 275 knot speed; on course at two-seven-zero—west. He squinted against the fog and grimaced. Then Larner heard the disappointing order from Colonel Bob Strickland, 3rd Group commander.

"This is Alpine Leader . . . Alpine leader. All units—abort! Abort and return to base!"

Larner scowled. For a full day he had waited for this opportunity and now it had been plucked from him. He was tempted to argue with his commanding officer, insist that they continue to the target. But Larner knew it was useless. Weather planes had reported clouds earlier and Colonel Upthegarde had complained about them when he reached the target with his 38th Group. Now the front was apparently closing in everything from the Solomons to the Admiralties, the entire Bismarck Archipelago. Visibility was reported at a mere 400 feet over the convoy, worse than it had been since the cloud front moved in yesterday.

Colonel Strickland ordered his pilots to climb to 7,000 feet, turn, and head home. He prayed that visibility would not be at zero by the time he brought his three squadrons of the 3rd Bomb Group back to Dobodura.

When Larner emerged above the clouds and squinted at the bright sun to the west, he cursed again to relieve his frustration. He had missed his chance to join the biggest strike of the Southwest Pacific war!

Chapter Nine

THE ENEMY IS MOTHER NATURE

By 1730 hours, the B-25's were tucked snugly into their revetment dispersal areas at Dobodura, but a heavy gloom permeated the base.

The bomber crews rode mutely in the jeeps that carried them back to their quarters, their heads bent in disappointment. Occasionally, an airman looked up and cursed the low-hanging overcast that caused him to miss out on New Guinea's most critical air campaign to date. Shocked ground crews fingered the cold .50 caliber barrels on aircraft, or looked at the still-loaded bomb bays, or rubbed the fuselages of the aborted planes. All personnel on the base felt terribly cheated.

Fifteen minutes after touchdown, Ed Larner, still in battle gear, slipped into the radio shack. The usual cluster of men were gathered about, listening to the garbled voices that intermittently broke through the static. The communications officer looked at Larner and gravely shook his head. "The convoy's regrouped and shifted direction. They're back on a two-four-six degree course and heading straight for Lae."

Larner merely sighed in his disappointment.

But Fifth Air Force was not remaining idle because of this setback from the fickle Southwest Pacific weather. Relay flights of Australian P-40's, staging from Wau and carrying belly tanks for extra range, continued to track the convoy. The Aussie pilots had patrolled for almost an hour before they were able to locate Kimura's convoy. It was still traveling west, although at a reduced speed of seven knots. Their current location was 148.1 east, 5.5 south. Nineteen of the Japanese ships were reported still afloat, with a cruiser towing a damaged transport. Other ships, those that had suffered superstructure damage, were proceeding under their own power.

Despite the growing dusk, General Whitehead had sent Australian Beauforts after the enemy ships. The light bombers were capable of making low-level torpedo attacks under the low cloud ceiling. At 1830 hours on the evening of 2 March, the radioman at the 90th Bomb Squadron heard the Australian flight leader.

"Okay, Maties, let's give 'er a go!"

Ed Larner had removed his flying gear and had stepped into the radio shack just as the first reports from the Aussie Beauforts came in.

Meanwhile, at one of the enlisted men's tents, Sergeant Joe Cardis had also removed his heavy flying gear. Then he flopped on a cot and stared up at the sloping canvas of his tent quarters. He yawned and stretched his legs. The crackle of loosening joints and stiff bones soothed him. He reached over to a small stand, an old ammo crate, and picked up a small pocketbook novel. But as he opened the first page a fellow gunner entered the tent.

The gunner urged Cardis to accompany him to evening chow. The mess cooks had prepared beef stew, with fresh meat from Brisbane and fresh vegetables from Australian farms. However, Cardis had lost his appetite. Like his *Spook* pilot, Ed Larner, he cursed the foul weather that had cheated him of the opportunity to attack the Japanese convoy. The young gunner could still see the huge pattern of 22 ships spread out over a wide patch of the Bismarck Sea—and he saw them getting away.

Cardis' companion tried to temper the young gunner's disappointment. "What's the difference? We wouldn't have done any better than the 38th Group."

"We would if we had skip bombs," Cardis answered. "We could come within 25 yards." Cardis beamed, his gray eyes alive now.

"But we didn't have skip bombs," Cardis' companion answered. Again he urged the *Spook* gunner to come to chow. After all, they didn't get fresh meat and vegetables every day. Cardis sighed, rose from his cot and followed his companion to the mess hall.

A hundred yards away Sal Dineo sat on his cot with a mixture of relief and disappointment. Two fellow airmen sat on opposite cots in the same tent. All three officers looked dejected, despite the mess hall menu of fresh beef stew. The fliers could only think of the aborted mission and the damned lousy weather that was holding them back.

A fourth officer stepped into the tent and the bitter look on his face forecast more bad news for the 90th Squadron airmen. The newcomer had been listening to the radio reports and they were not good. He told Dineo and the others that the Australian Beauforts had failed in their attempt to hurt the convoy with torpedoes. They had only scored some minor hits on a destroyer but they had not even slowed the Japanese warship. The officer's comments merely confirmed what most Southwest Pacific pilots already knew: if Japanese helmsmen could deftly avoid high-altitude bombing, these same helmsmen were equally adept at avoiding torpedo attacks. Their antiaircraft gunners had shown remarkable and brazen courage in the face of low-level torpedo planes. They had usually responded with accurate fire, so disturbing to torpedo planes that the attackers often dropped their torpedoes prematurely.

All four airmen sensed the same dire possibility: the Japanese convoy would reach Lae almost intact—unless the weather broke again.

Three of the officers left the tent for chow, but Dineo refused to go. He slumped on his cot and looked up at the canvas cover over him. He closed his eyes, but the image of the huge convoy remained clear in his mind. He shook his head to chase away the mental picture, but suddenly the thought of Wau arose—the imminent danger there. And he wondered about Lae and Salamaua and Madang. What could they expect tomorrow if the huge convoy unloaded at Lae?

How many added bombing and attack missions would such new Japanese pressure force upon them? Heavier support, more dangerous strikes—and, perhaps, all in a losing cause.

Sal Dineo, like Cardis, also felt compassion for his bitterly disappointed commander. Unlike Ed Larner, Dineo had not suffered the devastations of Java and the Philippines and New Guinea. He had not been subjected to the awesome enemy power during those first hairy months of the war. Then the lieutenant almost laughed. The very weather that had so often served as a third line of defense for the harried Allies had now turned against them.

Dineo finally rose from his cot, left the tent, and hurried towards the mess hall. Perhaps a good meal of beef stew might help him to forget. He tried to ignore the low, swift-moving overcast, but its gray dampness brushed his face with a cool, annoying, moistness.

ONE HUNDRED FIFTY MILES NORTHWEST, in the nestled Wau base, the heavy black and gray clouds had shrouded the surrounding slopes and peaks with a dense mist. The airstrip looked like a length of gray highway. The adjacent kunai plains resembled the eerie moors of England's misty lowlands. The dark overcast had paled the green foliage of trees in front of the defense perimeter, and the jungle had disappeared in a whisping fog rather than in a deep green.

Lance Corporal Lloyd York and Private Allan Caruthers, two infantrymen of the Australian Kanga Force, had been sitting in their sandpit machine gun nest all afternoon. They had been playing two up, a coin-tossing game with two-pence coins to while away the time. Thus far, Private Caruthers had lost two bobs to his companion, but they had suspended their game for the moment to meditate again in a mixture of fear and hope on the progress or lack of progress of the Japanese convoy.

The two men reflected the feelings of other Australian troops. They, above all others in Allied Papua, and even Australia itself, could visualize the terror that might pour out of the gloomy jungles in front of them if the convoy reached its destination. They had already repulsed one *banzai* attack, thanks to aircraft support. The Kanga Force Aussies were too realistic to assume that they could beat back a second such charge out of the jungles, particularly if the charging enemy consisted of fresh, fully equipped troops, newly arrived in Lae, only fifty air miles away.

York and Caruthers were part of a three-man machine gun team. The third man, Private Bill Herford, had spent most of the afternoon running back and forth to the Wau radio shack to pick up the latest word on the Allied air strikes against the convoy. Thus far, Herford had only returned to the machine gun pit with disappointing news: The 38th Bomb Group had sunk a cruiser and tanker, but not much else. Prospects had heightened when the 3rd Bomb Group, with a full complement of three squadrons, went after the Lae Resupply Convoy. But, their thirty-one B-25's and fifteen A-20's had been forced to turn back because of bad weather. Now, late this afternoon, the Aussies' own airmen with their Beauforts from the 9th Operational Group had taken a shot at the convoy, attacking under the clouds with torpedoes. Maybe their own people had accomplished something.

Caruthers and York stiffened anxiously in their sandpit when Private Bill Herford again ran across the open Wau terrain from the radio shack to join them. Sweat rolled down the face of Herford, despite the growing coolness of early evening, and his chest heaved with heavy gasps after the long run.

"Well?" Lance Corporal York asked eagerly.

"Nothin', nothin' at all," Herford shook his head. "The blokes at comm say our Beaus didn't do a thing with their torpedoes, not a thing. And we lost a plane, we did."

"Nothing? Nothing at all?" York asked in disbelief.

Herford sighed and slumped in the gunpit. "The Yanks can't get 'em and and Beaus can't hurt 'em. The Nip convoy'll be in the Solomon Sea by morning, and sometime late tomorrow those bloody Japs will be in Lae."

The three Aussies fell silent. These defenders at Wau had nothing more to say. They simply stared at the dense jungles in front of them, quiet now except for the occasional shrieks of lorrie birds. Then, as if resigned to the inevitable, Caruthers cocked the machine gun and aimed the weapon at the dense jungle growth.

FIFTY MILES FROM WAU, at the Japanese garrison in Lae, a radio messenger hurriedly entered the Eighteenth Army Headquarters bungalow of General Hatazo Adachi. The general, of course, was aboard the Lae Resupply Convoy. General Toru Okabe had been temporarily occupying Adachi's quarters. Okabe was just settling down to his evening meal with some of his staff. No Japanese enlisted man, or even officer subordinates for that matter, dared to interrupt the general at his meal unless the 102nd Brigade commander asked for him. But General Okabe had done just that: asked for every radio report, even if such reports came in every five minutes. Like everyone else in the Southwest Pacific, Okabe, too, wanted the latest word on the progress of the convoy—and he wanted it immediately. So he looked eagerly at the soldier as the messenger rushed into his quarters with a slip of paper in his hand.

"All continues to go well, General Okabe," the messenger said. "The heavy nimbus clouds have returned to linger for yet another day, and the stalwart Kimura maintains a steady course for Lae." The soldier looked at his watch. "He is less than a day from joining us."

"And there have been no further losses?" the general asked.

"In vain did a squadron of Australian torpedo planes attack the honorable Kimura. They inflicted but slight damage, while our gunners shot down several of the bombers." (This report was grossly exaggerated.)

General Okabe nodded. "Nineteen vessels will assuredly reach us tomorrow." Then the 102nd Brigade commander looked at his staff, who had paused in their supper. "The gods have favored us."

Okabe now rose from his dinner table and walked outside the bungalow to stare first into the dense jungles beyond Lae and then at the heavy clouds boiling overhead, so close to the ground that he could almost touch them. A staff member was suddenly next to him and he too stared at the enmeshed foliage of the dense trees beyond Lae.

"Before the first buds of cherry blossoms seek the sunlight of spring," the aide said, "we shall destroy the cancer at Wau."

"Banzai," Okabe answered softly with a grin.

Throughout the Japanese base at Lae, a festive atmosphere had gripped the garrison. Exhilaration had replaced despair; anticipation had replaced uncertainty. Troops swaggered through the township in elated groups.

Sake flowed liberally after the traditional mess of rice and fish. The excited soldiers urged on the dock crews, and with each new effort they rewarded those preparing jetties and barges with *sake*. Cheers and renewed efforts followed.

The troops sensed a resurgence of those early months when Japan rolled through the Far East like an unchecked prairie fire.

The elation had spread to other Eighteenth Army units in Finschafen, Madang, and Wewak. And far across the Solomon Sea, in Rabaul, Commander-in-Chief Hitoshi Imamura ate his late evening meal with a gusto shared by his staff members. They toasted the daring and persistent Kimura, not once or twice, but three times. In these hours, when the fate of the Southwest Pacific war hung in the balance, Kimura had thus far responded brilliantly. The "Eel of the Pacific," with cunning and brazenness, had successfully defied almost all of the Fifth Air Force. Perhaps Mother Nature, impressed by Kimura's efforts, had rewarded the Lae Resupply Convoy commander by again spreading a protective cover of nimbus clouds over the convoy.

And while 200 American planes remained grounded, except for the tracking P-40's and Australian PBY reconnaissance planes, the Lae Resupply Convoy plodded on. Kimura had ignored the snooping Warhawks and Catalinas since they offered no threat to his fleet. Occasionally, however, Japanese ack-ack gunners sent the searching planes scurrying back into the clouds with a burst of pom-pom antiaircraft fire. The Japanese sailors and soldiers had ample reasons to feel safe and confident at the moment. Both weather and time were on their side.

AT PORT MORESBY, A CONTRASTING MOOD prevailed. Evening chow had passed unnoticed in the rickety hotel. Clerks sat in glum silence at desks. Communications officers winced with each fresh message, since new reports only compounded the disappointment. Weathermen saw no break in the foul weather front. The nimbus clouds continued to thicken and expand while the ceiling dropped lower. By 1900, meteorologists estimated the depth of the massive cloud front at well over a mile.

General Ennis Whitehead's face reflected the mood of not only Fifth Air Force ADVON personnel, but of Allied men everywhere in Papua. Pain radiated from Whitehead's eyes, frustration had cut crevices around his mouth, and anger had tightened his lips until they looked chafed. Pappy Gunn and two staff officers, stoney-faced and silent, stood across the desk from Whitehead. They dared not speak for fear of irritating the general further. They already knew that the aggravation brought on by the continuing foul weather had already aroused Whitehead to an emotional pitch.

Finally, after looking at the huge Bismarck Archipelago map, General Whitehead spoke in sharp, quick phrases to his staff.

He continually asked about the convoy's speed, only to receive the same answer: seven knots. He inquired about the weather, only to receive the same appalling news: there was no change, except for the worst. Ceiling was now at 300 feet and still dropping. Whitehead suggested the possible use of A-20's with parachute frag bombs. Here, however, his staff mustered the courage to disagree. Thirty-pound frag bombs would be the same as throwing rocks at a motor launch. Whitehead agreed and quickly dropped the suggestion.

Whitehead queried if they could attack the convoy after it reached Lae. Maybe, came the response, but the sky would be black with a protective cover of Zeros. And they would have to catch the ships in the harbor before they unloaded.

All four officers in Whitehead's quarters at the Port Moresby Hotel, despite their conjectures on what to do, understood clearly that time was on the side of the Japanese so long as the weather held out. They knew that by tomorrow evening, at the latest, fresh Japanese troops would be in Lae, and that by the next day, these same troops would be on the way to Wau. There would be more of them now, better equipped, rested and eager. General Adachi might even send a part of this new force through the jungles to attack Gona, just beyond the Allies' strategic Dobodura airbase.

So General Whitehead, despite his irritation, and despite all the options suggested by his staff, did the only thing he could do. He kept his bombers and fighters loaded and ready for a quick takeoff in the event there arose a new chance to hit the convoy. Realistically, however, Whitehead knew that no strike could be made before dawn.

"General," a voice suddenly came over his intercom, "can we bring you some dinner?"

The question apparently hit Whitehead the wrong way, and he swatted the intercom on his desk with the back of his right hand. The case skidded off the desk, but one of the staff colonels alertly caught it in mid-air.

Colonel Pappy Gunn leaned over the general's desk. "We still have one ace in the hole. The skip bombers. I'd like to authorize a skip bomb attack by the 3rd Group in the morning. With your permission, sir."

But Whitehead shook his head. "Too dangerous. We've only experimented with the skip bomb and we don't know what the hell would happen if we tried it for real. Maybe the technique worked all right here in Moresby or at Oro Bay, but there weren't any Japanese antiaircraft gunners and eager beaver Zeke pilots shooting back at them."

"General," Gunn said softly, "if this weather holds—and the meteorologists say it will—that goddamned convoy is going into Lae. There's only one chance to stop them—the skip bomb."

"I'll think about it," Ennis Whitehead gestured.

BUT PAPPY GUNN DECIDED TO MOVE on his own. He hitched a ride on the evening mail plane out of Port Moresby for the short hop over the Owen Stanley hump to Dobodura. By 2100, he was sitting in the 3rd Bomb Group operations shack with Major Ed Larner, Major Glen Clark of the 89th Squadron, and Colonel Bob Strickland, 3rd Bomb Group commander. At once, Gunn suggested the use of skip bombs against the Lae Resupply Convoy. The skip bombers would need less than a 100-foot ceiling, and they could come in under the clouds.

Colonel Bob Strickland quickly agreed with Gunn. Like Ed Larner, Strickland had spent too many months in the Southwest Pacific as a bomber pilot and he had experienced the devastation of Japanese superiority in arms, men, planes, and naval units. Strickland remembered his arrival in Chartres Towers, Australia, a year ago when the 3rd Group's B-25's were the only available medium bombers against the Japanese in the Southwest Pacific.

The colonel recalled the long flights from Chartres Towers to Port Moresby where they staged for raids on Lae, Buna, and Gasmata, New Britain. Quite often Japanese Zeros would wait in the skies over Moresby for the B-25's to come into Eight-Mile Drome. The Zekes would then dive at the 3rd Group aircraft as the Mitchells tried to land and load up for a bomb run to the other side of the Owen Stanleys. The colonel had seen 3rd Group crews fall victim to Japanese fighter pilots or battle fatigue. He had seen his aircraft become worn-out hulks or riddled junk for lack of repair and service.

Strickland appreciated the growing strength of the Allied air force in New Guinea during the past several months. The last thing the colonel wanted was a reversal of these gains. The convoy plying towards Lae threatened just such a possibility and he was determined to take any chance, no matter how dangerous, to stop the Japanese armada.

Thus, when Pappy Gunn suggested the use of the skip bomb, Strickland never hesitated. "You don't have to convince me, Pappy."

Major Ed Larner and Major Glen Clark quickly agreed.

"But the general isn't sure," Gunn said.

"I'll convince him," Strickland promised. "I'll go all the way to MacArthur if I have to! They can court-martial me for going over their heads, but if we get that goddamned convoy, a court-martial will be worth it!"

Only an hour later, on the evening of 2 March 1943, Colonel Strickland assembled the airmen of his 90th and 89th Squadrons. He told them he planned to hit the Japanese convoy with skip bombs in the morning. "However, we're only asking for volunteers. Nobody has to fly on a skip bomb run if he doesn't want to."

Nobody declined.

Pappy Gunn then told the airmen that General Whitehead had not really approved the skip bomb strike. At best, they could only prepare for such a strike and wait for an okay from Port Moresby. However, Bob Strickland showed more determination. He told his airmen they *would* go. He had already ordered ordnance men to install the five-second fuses on 500 pounders, altering the conventional bombs to skip bombs.

"I'll take full responsibility," Colonel Strickland informed his men. "You'll follow the pattern you learned in Port Moresby and Oro Bay. The B-25's will go in first. Then, Major Clark will come in with his A-20's." The colonel looked at Ed Larner. "I wish I could go along, but I didn't train in this technique. So the mission is yours, Ed. You lead."

"Remember what I told you," Colonel Gunn cautioned, "fifteen seconds apart, fifteen seconds. And be careful. The ceiling over that convoy might be as low as two hundred feet by the time you get there, maybe lower. Play it just like we practiced—in pairs, fifteen seconds apart. They'll never expect this new technique. They'll veer and expose port or starboard beams. That's just what you want. Then, you can sock four or five holes into the hull. They won't be able to seal off any compartments before they sink."

"And like I said," Strickland reminded, "I'll take the responsibility."

He then ordered his men to get a good night's sleep. The crews of the 90th and 89th Squadrons were to be out on the strip by 0400 for briefing and—hopefully—over the target by 0600.

When the meeting broke up, Strickland put through a call to General Whitehead. The general did not appreciate the call for he had just fallen asleep, his first catnap in two days. But he soon calmed down and listened to the 3rd Group commander.

Strickland told the Fifth Air Force ADVON commander that his 89th and 90th Squadrons were going out at dawn to hit the convoy with skip bombs. When Whitehead balked, Strickland reminded him, just as Gunn did, that they had no other choice. So long as this severe weather front continued to hang over the Bismarck Archipelago, conventional bombing runs would be ineffective. Torpedo planes had also failed. Pappy Gunn had approved the skip bombers, the 3rd Group pilots were eager to skip bomb, and he himself wholeheartedly concurred.

As Whitehead still hesitated, Strickland continued his pressing argument. He reminded Whitehead that the convoy would reach Lae sometime tomorrow, and that it was probably close to the Dampier Strait now. However, Whitehead still held back. This would be an attack against a real target, not a shoot-out against derelicts in Merrick Bay. He could not afford to endanger a single plane on experiment.

"General," Strickland finally spoke bluntly, "my guys are going out with skip bombs at first light tomorrow. The only way you'll stop them is to send a battalion of MP's up here to Dobodura, arrest them, and throw them all into the goddam stockade until Kimura makes it to Lae."

Whitehead was stunned into silence for a moment, but then a sudden, unexpected laugh erupted from his throat. The laugh was so pronounced that the guffaws astonished the clerks in the ramshackle orderly rooms of Fifth Air Force Headquarters. Nobody had heard such laughter from General Whitehead since the Battle of the Coral Sea; and they were shocked to hear it now in view of the general's mood of the past two days. However, the laugh brought grins from the personnel working at headquarters. Whatever the reason for his outburst, the change in General Whitehead was a pleasant surprise.

"Strickland," Whitehead said, after his laugh subsided, "I haven't got a battalion of MP's to arrest you guys. I haven't even got a platoon of 'em. And even if I did, I haven't got a plane to fly 'em to Dobodura. So I guess there isn't much I can do."

"Yes sir," Strickland answered elatedly.

"And good luck." Whitehead suddenly spoke softly and somberly.

Chapter Ten

KIMURA'S GAMBLE

Only an hour before midnight on the evening of 2 March, the night had turned chilly on the Bismarck Sea. Admiral Kimura had retired to the wheelhouse of the *Shirayuki* for a little warmth, and he stood pressed against a window, squinting at the black outlines of the other ships under his charge. In the pitch black that enveloped the open sea, no moon and no stars were visible. Only a misty gloom hung between the shadowy clouds overhead and the murky surface of the water. Even aboard the cruiser itself, a silent darkness prevailed. The ship seemed almost deserted, for Kimura's sailors on night duty worked in quiet seclusion on this last lap of the 1600 hours watch. Other sailors had retired for the night.

Inside the wheelhouse, diagonal from Kimura, the helmsman kept the big cruiser on a steady course while the bridge assistant silently stood by. Occasionally, both men shuttled their glances between the dark emptiness before them and the lonely figure of their admiral standing at the window. Both the helmsman and the assistant felt a euphoria for the "Eel of the Pacific." They knew the admiral was relaxed now, at ease, and enjoying the cruise. The foul weather, holding fast, had eased the perils and frustrations of the past two days. No doubt, by this time tomorrow, Admiral Kimura would be the honored guest of General Adachi in the Japanese base at Lae.

From the wheelhouse, Admiral Kimura heard only two sounds: the steady, swishing wash of the cruiser's prow and the constant drone of P-40's and PYB's overhead. The monotonous swish of the sea and the equally monotonous drone of the Allied reconnaissance planes might have served as a lullaby to hasten sleep. However, antiaircraft guns from the warships occasionally interrupted the humdrum refrains of the night with short, deafening barrages. The infrequent b-blooms of ack-ack not only shattered the quiet, somber night, but also ignited screams from the shadowing planes as they darted into the dark clouds for cover.

Finally, Admiral Kimura retreated from the window and turned to the helmsman. "At what point are we now?"

The helmsman's companion stiffened before he scampered across the wheelhouse to look at the chart. "148 west by 5.9 south. At any moment now, Admiral, we will make our turn into the Dampier Strait."

"If he is still awake, ask Captain Tishayuna to meet me in the chart room in five minutes," Kimura said.

"Yes, Admiral."

Several minutes later, Admiral Kimura, Captain Tishayuna, and several other ship's officers gathered about a map table in the chart room of the cruiser. "I am told," Kimura said, "that we are approaching the Dampier Strait, if we have not already reached it. I propose, Gentlemen, that we avoid the Dampier Strait altogether."

A low chain of mumbles radiated through the chart room.

Kimura explained his proposal, a plan that had apparently jelled his mind as he stood in the wheelhouse of his cruiser in quiet meditation. The admiral pointed out that the Allied spy planes had been tracking them for several hours. They, as well as Fifth Air Force Headquarters in Port Moresby, expected the convoy to soon turn into the Dampier Strait. They expected the convoy to sail through the strait during the night and begin their run across the Solomon Sea to Lae early tomorrow morning.

Should the weather break, Kimura warned his staff, swarms of Allied bombers would seek out the convoy at first light. The enemy aircraft would streak northward to the exit of the Dampier Strait to find them. And even if the foul weather held, as expected, the Allies might again attack the convoy with torpedo planes or even low-level fighter planes and light bombers acting as dive bombers. The Allies might even now be sending submarines to the exit of the Dampier Strait. To lessen the chance of further enemy attacks, Kimura repeated his proposal to stay away from the Dampier Strait altogether.

"What are your thoughts, Admiral?" Captain Tishayuna asked.

Kimura suggested they turn as expected into the Dampier Strait, but then they would exercise another ruse against the observation planes. They would fool the Allies into believing they had gone into the Dampier Strait. But once they made their turn, they would shake off the planes and lose themselves again.

The convoy would remain in the Dampier Strait for less than an hour and then unleash a heavy barrage of antiaircraft fire on the Allied planes that were tracking the convoy. Although three PBY's and a half dozen P-40's made up the complement, only a few came under the clouds at a time, generally no more than three. The Allied pilots were squeamish because gunnery crews in the convoy had been amusing themselves by throwing infrequent ack-ack fire at them, chasing the planes back into the clouds. Kimura had noticed that after each antiaircraft burst had chased the planes off, the Allied observers stayed out of sight for some time before venturing out of the clouds again.

The admiral suggested that this time they keep up an incessant ack-ack barrage. Such fire would keep the planes out of sight for a long time. And, while the reconnaissance planes remained in the refuge of the clouds, the convoy would veer 90 degrees, steam out of the Dampier Strait, and sail west at full speed towards Undoi Island. By the time the Allied planes came out of the clouds again, the convoy would be gone.

Kimura further suggested that the spy plane pilots would not be suspicious. They had already been subjected to antiaircraft fire throughout the evening and they would simply believe that Japanese gunners had exhausted their patience and had now decided to chase them off completely. The pilots, when they finally came out off the clouds again and saw the convoy gone, would assume they had lost the convoy in the darkness while they were hiding in the clouds from ack-ack fire. The Allies would simply resume the search at daylight, certain the convoy was passing through the Dampier Strait during the nighttime hours.

But, Kimura emphasized, the convoy would be on a completely different course, far from the Dampier Strait. The Lae Resupply Convoy would be nearing the Vitiaz Strait by morning, far to the west. Before the Allied planes could find them again, they would be through the Vitiaz Strait, across the Huon Gulf, and inside Lae Harbor. This would especially be true with the thick, low-hanging cloud cover that would hamper any Allied search operations.

Captain Tishayuna bowed slightly before the admiral. "An ingenious plan, Kimura-*san*. Such a strategy will most certainly assure the success of our mission."

"Relay instructions to all ship commanders by blinker signals," Kimura said.

The admiral glanced at his watch: 2335 hours. "We shall celebrate the approach of a new day with a fireworks display, the likes of which has never been seen over the Bismarck Sea."

At precisely 2345, the Lae Resupply Convoy made its wide turn into the Dampier Strait and sailed southwestward for half an hour. Then, at 0115, the dark misty night over the surface of the Bismarck Sea exploded in blinding, deafening b-bloom from antiaircraft fire. For a full hour the exploding flashes and thundering booms of ack-ack shook the night. Black wads of flak puffed like dark paper balls in the low-hanging clouds.

The six P-40's and three PBY's of the Australian 16th Reconn-Search Squadron had quickly scampered away and flown outward and upward for miles to escape the blistering barrage. The pilots had suspected nothing, simply assuming—as Kimura guessed—that the Japanese had decided to drive them off. And while the reconn planes scattered, the signal came from the *Shirayuki:* Veer 90 degrees and steer straight westward at a full ten knots towards Undoi Island. The steady ack-ack barrage kept the

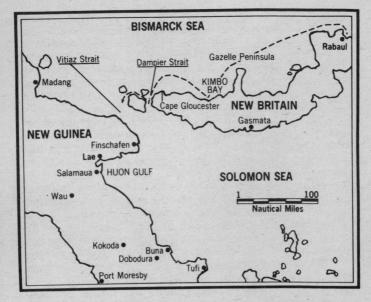

Map 5: Kimura backtracks from Dampier Strait to Vitiaz Strait.

Australian reconn planes out of sight for nearly an hour and by 0205 hours, 3 March, the convoy was well on its way to the Vitiaz Strait—far to the west.

It was nearly 0230 hours before the reconnaissance planes ventured out of the clouds. The pilots saw nothing. However, the Allied observers were unconcerned. They had only lost their quarry in the dark night. The planes continued southward through the Dampier Strait to locate the convoy. But they soon reached the Solomon Sea without a sign of the convoy.

" 'Igh Point, 'Igh Point," one of the PBY observers called Fifth Air Force, "Your bloody Nips really put on a pom-pom show; chased us to Limbo, they did. We last spotted 'em a half hour inside the Dampier Strait, but we can't find 'em now in these dark channels. But they'll bloody sure be comin' out of the strait around daylight. You can pick 'em up again then."

NORMALLY, THREE CRASH TRUCKS, two ambulances, and a few of the ground crew personnel watched aircraft leave on a mission. However, the runways at Dobodura at 0500, 3 March 1943, were jammed with vehicles and men—like the Rose Bowl before kick-off time. They had emerged from the tree-covered campsites about the airdrome, they had come out of the line shacks and repair tents, and they had wandered over from the revetment areas. Not only had every airman in the 89th and 90th Squadrons crowded the 60-by-3,000-yard bomber strip, but also those from the 38th Group and service squadrons. Even units of ground troops had filtered up from Buna, over the dirt-hewn road to be at the airfield.

The sudden ignition of B-25 and A-20 engines at 0430 that drew the personnel at Dobodura and Buna to the airfield had been most unusual. Where could they be going in this foul weather? The thick overcast had not thinned a yard. To the contrary, the clouds had grown denser and the ceiling had dropped lower. Since last evening all planes had been grounded. So with the bursts of aircraft engines, men knew instinctively that something big was happening.

When the high-pitched whines of P-38's also reverberated across Dobodura, a half hour after the bombers, this curiosity was compounded. Every man here, whether an air group commander or a supply clerk, knew the pattern: bombers were going on a mission with fighter escorts. On this bleak, weather-closed morning only one target could spur a combat flight in these near impossible flying conditions—the Japanese convoy plodding towards Lae.

As Larner's eleven B-25's, in pairs, roared down the runway and lifted skyward, the airfield spectators sensed doubt. The aircraft disappeared into the misty overcast only moments after takeoff. However, by the time Major Glen Clark's fifteen A-20's had taken off, fact had replaced rumor. The 3rd Bomb Group aircraft would attempt a low-level strike against the convoy with a new technique—the skip bomb. Doubt changed to sudden hope. The hundreds of eager faces at Dobodura prayed that the daring airmen aboard the twenty-six planes could bring about a miracle.

As silently as the other spectators, Colonels Strickland and Gunn watched the takeoff. From the bomber strip control tower, they counted each pair of B-25's as the planes roared past them before hoisting themselves into the air. And the officers watched Major Glen Clark and his fifteen A-20's, as the Havocs also sped down the runway and into the low-hanging clouds.

When the last A-20 lifted off the bomber strip at 0630, Pappy Gunn lit his cigar and turned to the 3rd Group commander. "Well, Colonel?"

"I was just thinking, Pappy," Strickland answered. "Fifty-three planes barely dented that convoy yesterday. Now we're sending in twenty-six. That's about a plane per ship."

"Colonel, do you know any prayers?"

"I've said a few in my time."

"Try some now," Gunn said. "A good prayer might give Larner and Clark the edge they need."

MAJOR ED LARNER STUDIED THE altimeter: 7,000 feet. Then he stared at the rising sun, relishing the contrast to the bleak gray of Dobodura's airstrip. In the clear blue, the wing B-25 of his lead diamond hung in sharp focus. Under him, the tops of the thick cloud cover resembled a field of shorn wool: clear, billowy, white.

Lieutenant Sal Dineo also stared from the *Spook*'s cabin, watching the same endless field of white puffs under him. And he too peered into the sun or studied the sky. The vivid blue reminded him of the peaceful landscape of his native Hudson Valley. The sky at early morning was a clear blue there, too, and the sun radiated the same gentle warmth with the approaching morning. Even the monotonous drone of the Mitchell's twin engines, whining now for more than thirty-five minutes, soothed him like a lullaby.

In the bubble, Sergeant Joe Cardis felt a sense of superiority. He was up here in the blue sky and sparkling sun while those back at Dobodura and Buna saw only the drab overcast. Cardis counted the parade of bombers behind him, the B-25 diamonds of his squadron and the A-20's stretching into the distance. The aircraft flew like hovering albatrosses gliding with the trade winds.

Cardis had forgotten the purpose of his flight, until suddenly the shapes of P-38's loomed from the east and settled a thousand feet above the bombers. The young sergeant bit his lips, then clutched the triggers of his twin machine guns.

"This is Alpine Leader, Alpine Leader," Larner spoke into

his radio. "We'll settle at 150. Repeat: settle at 150."

The latest weather data had reported a two- to three-hundred-foot ceiling over the Solomon Sea and Larner considered one hundred and fifty feet a safe altitude under the clouds.

Within moments, the line of bombers, eleven B-25's and fifteen A-20's, had disappeared into the thick clouds. Cardis felt uneasy. He could feel the Mitchell dropping and he wondered if they would hit daylight before they hit the sea itself.

Inside the cabin, Sal Dineo watched the altimeter needle drop: 4.0, 3.5, 3.0. Then he squinted at the enshrouding mist where companion aircraft were hazy black silhouettes. He looked at Major Larner, but the commander's face was blank. Dineo stiffened in his seat and closed his eyes. A moment later, he felt the B-25 jerk and level off. His entire body relaxed. They had come under the clouds. Now, instead of the lazy white puffs under him, Dineo saw the choppy waters of the sea.

The water reflected an angry blue hue and exploding white caps. The engines were roaring again instead of purring. And ahead, the copilot saw only a gray horizon, a monotonous hoary sameness. Dineo could sense the atmosphere of war.

But then, at 0730, less than a half hour from the expected target area, a shocking order came from Colonel Bob Strickland to Major Ed Larner. "Alpine Leader, abort mission; abort mission and return to base."

Larner was stunned. He stared in astonishment at Dineo, who was equally stunned.

"You've got to be kidding!" the 90th Squadron major cried into his radio. "We're only a half hour from target."

"There is no target," Strickland said. "They lost the convoy again. It isn't anywhere near the Dampier Strait, so get your ass home—on the double!"

It was later, after the B-25's and A-20's had landed at Dobodura at about 0830 hours that Ed Larner and the other 3rd Bomb Group airmen learned the full truth. Since the first bands of daylight, at 0430 this morning, nearly a dozen reconnaissance planes had been searching the Dampier strait and the northern areas of the Solomon sea. They had also scoured Rooke Island, the southern coast of New Britain all the way to Gasmata, the Cape Gloucester area north of the Dampier Strait, and the coastal areas of Rooke Island. The search planes this morning had scoured to the last moment before suggesting an abort for the skip bomb mission.

A few of the reconnaissance planes, the long-range PBY's, had even searched as far north as Undoi Island and as far west as Madang. Nobody had seen the convoy anywhere near the exit of the Dampier Strait, the expected location for the 3rd Group skip bombers.

Only when the searchers were sure did they radio Fifth Air Force. And only then did Fifth Air Force order Colonel Strickland to call back his bombers. It was then, too, that a growling General Whitehead suddenly realized the truth. Last night's hour long ack-ack attack against the reconnaissance planes had been a ruse so the Lae Resupply Convoy could lose itself again.

When Larner met again with Strickland, he frowned. "What do we do now?"

"Nothing," the colonel answered. "We just sit and wait and hope they relocate the convoy."

Ed Larner looked up at the low-hanging clouds, a part of the dense weather front that continued its stranglehold on the Bismarck Archipelago. Twice the weather had been the culprit. Larner cursed the gloomy skies.

At Port Moresby, General Whitehead had reverted to his irritable self. No belly laughs erupted from his throat now and no smiles widened his face. He could only stare in anger at the large map of the Bismarck Archipelago on the wall of his inner office. He could only scowl when radiomen brought him the same report: no sign of the convoy; or he could only curse when meteorologists brought him the same bad news: no change in the weather.

"The sly bastard!" Whitehead cursed, obviously referring to Admiral Kimura.

Whitehead knew good weather would enable the search planes to find the convoy in relatively short order. On a clear day, the reconnaissance pilots could fly PBY's at high altitudes and cover a dozen square miles of sea in one panoramic glance. But, the foxy commander of the enemy convoy had correctly guessed that the low-hanging clouds over the Bismarck Archipelago had made impossible any quick, wide search.

At 0530 this morning, even as the 3rd Group skip bombers

had been taking off, Whitehead had called on naval units, submarines and PT boats to reconnoiter the Solomon Sea and the Dampier Strait. But thus far the navy had been no more successful in their quest than had the reconn planes.

Aboard the *Shirayuki*, however, Admiral Kimura enjoyed a simple breakfast of *shiromiso*, rice, and *nori* (seaweed). His convoy was now steaming south through the Vitiaz Strait after passing between Rooke and Undoi Islands during the night. By afternoon on this dull, gray March 3, he would be within 50 knots of Lae. By late afternoon or early evening he would disembark his soldiers and unload his supplies.

Kimura had indeed shown uncanny skill in his cat-and-mouse contest with General Whitehead. He had used the foul Southwest Pacific weather to full advantage, twice secreting his huge convoy from the prying eyes of American and Australian reconnaissance. And this time it appeared that Admiral Kimura had fatally checkmated General Whitehead.

But Kimura had made one bizarre error. He had sent a request to the 7th Fighter Command in Lae: Aircraft from Lae should be on full alert to cover the convoy as the armada completed the last dangerous lap through Huon Gulf, within spitting distance of Allied bombers at Dobodura. The request was a most logical one, as any military strategist would agree. Huon Gulf *was* within range of every Allied aircraft in New Guinea, and air cover here could be a vital necessity. Yet, the decision to alert the Japanese 7th Fighter Command in Lae, amazingly, would prove fatal for the "Eel of the Pacific."

Chapter Eleven

ROUND 2: SKIP BOMB ATTACK

One of the curiosities of the Allied air command in New Guinea was the almost independent status of fighter plane units. If a P-38 or P-40 or Aussie Beaufighter squadron had no commitment to escort bombers, the pursuit squadron commander could usually get permission to launch his own sortie mission. On the fortunate arrival of the 49th Fighter Group planes to stop General Okabe at Wau, for example, the fighter unit had been on a self-directed strike against Salamaua.

The Japanese always presented small, worthwhile targets. They often moved troop barges or supply barges along the coastal waters, or they trucked men and supplies along the jungle trails or over open kunai fields. And Japanese service troops constantly built camps, repaired runways, serviced planes, or carried on other routine jobs. These day-to-day logistics activities offered good opportunities for fighter plane harassment. The pursuit aircraft could conduct straf- ing missions or light bomb runs with small wing bombs, napalm, or frag clusters. Or the fighter planes might be lucky enough to meet a flight of Zero or Hamp (Mitsubishi II) fighters for a good aerial dogfight.

Most fighter pilots were young, eager, and adventurous—always spoiling for a fight.

Since the Allied fighter plane units usually hounded the enemy from minimum altitudes, weather conditions rarely concerned them. So the fighter pilots did not worry about a long-hanging cloud front.

The Australian air base at Tufi, 20 miles east of Buna, housed the 75th and 77th Fighter Squadrons along with the light bomber squadrons of the RAAF 9th Operational Group. On the gray morning of March 3, 1943, with all bombers grounded, the squadron leaders of these two fighter units decided to make a few sorties up the coast of New Guinea. (They were not involved in the escort duty with the American skip bombers.) The two Australian fighter squadrons would hunt for small targets in the Salamaua, Lae, and Finschafen areas, and perhaps even further up the coast and across the Solomon Sea to New Britain. They might hit barges or troop concentrations, or they might run into a good dogfight with Japanese Zeros. Allied fighter pilots loved such dogfights, especially on an even basis, since the Allied pilots were superior to Japanese fighter pilots, primarily because of better training.

At about 1100 hours, while all Allied bomb groups remained grounded, Australian squadron leader Bill Archer of the 75th Squadron led a flight of eight P-40's up the coast towards Lae, seeking worthwhile targets. The leader of the 77th Squadron took his nine P-40's across the Solomon Sea to hunt around the Gasmata, New Britain, area.

Archer and his pilots found Salamaua quiet, but at Lae dozens of Japanese service troops were preparing dock facilities and barges in the harbor. Bill Archer was not surprised, since he knew the Japanese convoy hoped to reach Lae sometime that afternoon. But the sight on the Lae airstrips *did* surprise him. Four squadrons of Zero fighters were sitting wing tip to wing tip, their ground crews loitering nearby. The aircraft were apparently ready to take off on short notice. Before Archer and other P-40 pilots could get a closer look, antiaircraft fire drove them off.

Squadron Leader Archer then led his flight westward to Finschafen, Madang, and Wewak where, like Salamaua, the areas were quiet. Curiously, Archer radioed the squadron leader of the 77th Squadron who had flown across the Solomon Sea to the New Guinea coast. Was there any activity there? No. At Cape Gloucester and Gasmata, Japanese aircraft were snugly parked in their revetment areas. So among the five Japanese air bases of Lae, Madang, Wewak, Cape Gloucester, and Gasmata, only the aircraft at Lae were primed for a quick takeoff. Why?

Squadron Leader Archer drew only one conclusion: the convoy was somewhere along the coast of the Huon Peninsula and the planes at Lae were preparing to escort it through Huon Gulf to its destination. Bill Archer radioed his group commander at Tufi, who relayed the Australian squadron leader's suspicions to General Whitehead in Port Moresby.

The report raised some fascinating questions, and Whitehead quickly convened his staff in his inner office to discuss the report from the Australian squadron leader. Why would Japanese aircraft be relatively idle at Madang, Gasmata, Cape Gloucester, and Wewak—and be fully alerted at Lae? If the Japanese convoy was crossing the Solomon Sea from the Dampier Strait, the aircraft at Gasmata and Cape Gloucester would certainly be on instant ready. If the convoy were heading west to Madang, the aircraft at Madang and Wewak would be on the ready. The 5th Air Force ADVON commander and his staff agreed with Bill Archer's suspicions. The wily Japanese convoy commander had apparently taken his convoy through the Vitiaz Strait instead of the Dampier Strait. He had then sailed southeast along the Huon Peninsula and he had alerted the aircraft at Lae to escort him through Huon Gulf and into Lae Harbor.

"We'd best start searching," one of the staff colonels said. "We can keep those Aussie P-40 pilots right where they are around the Vitiaz Strait."

But Whitehead did not answer. Instead, he stared intently at his wall map of the Bismarck Archipelago. Then he poked a finger on Lae before he turned to Pappy Gunn. "Pappy, can anybody besides the 3rd Group make an air strike right away?"

"We might be grounded," Gunn answered, "but everybody's still on alert. We've got about 20 Bostons and Beauforts at Tufi and about a dozen B-25's of the 38th Group in Dobodura ready to go. And, of course, we've got our heavies here in Moresby."

"I think we'll need to gamble," Whitehead grinned. "I want those Aussie and 38th Group aircraft loaded with frag clusters and napalms for a low-level stroke. Then I want them over the Huon Gulf, but I don't want them to do anything but hang over the gulf until we give them the signal to hit those grounded aircraft at Lae."

If the staff wondered about Whitehead's strategy, the general soon explained. Whitehead believed that if the convoy was indeed skirting the coast of the Huon Peninsula, the fighters at Lae would take to the air the moment the convoy was sighted again by Allied reconnaissance planes. Swarms of Zeros would be hanging over the convoy by the time the 3rd Group skip bombers reached the target area. Fifth Air Force could muster no more than 40 or 50 fighter planes to escort the skip bombers and waiting Zeros might knock the bombers into the sea.

The Allies had to minimize Japanese interceptor attacks on the skip bombers. Whitehead suggested that the Aussie 9th and American 38th loiter over Huon Gulf until the P-40's spotted the convoy—assuming they did. The fighter pilots would then radio the 9th and 38th who would immediately head for the Lae Airfield and hit the alerted Zeros on the ground. Lae would only be a short distance away and the attack force could get there within fifteen or twenty minutes.

Whitehead believed that as soon as Admiral Kimura noted that Allied reconn planes had sighted him again, he would radio Lae to send out the Zero escorts. However, the 9th and 38th would hit Lae before the Zeros could respond. The Japanese would not send up their fighters that quickly, since they would logically believe that Allied attack planes would need at least an hour or more to take off from Dobodura and reach the convoy.

"But the whole operation has to be timed perfectly," Whitehead warned. "If we hit Lae too soon, the Japanese will send planes from their other bases. Their other bases are a lot closer to the Huon Peninsula than our own Dobodura base. Japanese fighter cover from these other bases might reach the convoy ahead of of our bombers."

"A good plan," Pappy Gunn said, "but will it work?"

True—would it work? Whitehead first had to find the Lae Resupply Convoy. He also had to make certain the Japanese did not become suspicious, and had to assume that a sky full of Japanese fighter escorts was not already hovering over the convoy. However, Whitehead's staff agreed with the general. They had to take the gamble.

"Even if we knock out some of that convoy before it reaches Lae," Gunn said, "it'll be better than nothing. I think this thing is going to work!"

So, Fifth Air Force headquarters in Port Moresby executed the plan.

But Squadron Leader Bill Archer balked when his 9th Operational Group commander relayed the Fifth Air Force request to him to remain in the Huon Peninsula area and hunt for the Japanese convoy. Archer's P-40's were low on fuel; they could barely fly back to Tufi. But the Australian group commander ordered Archer to fly to Wau, refuel, and then begin the search for the convoy. Both Squadron Leader Archer and the squadron leader of the 77th headed for Wau.

By 1300 hours, 3 March 1943, the two Australian fighter squadrons had refueled at Wau and were off again. Then, at only 1330 hours in the early afternoon, General Whitehead's first wish came true. Three P-40's searching east of Finschafen found their quarry. Nineteen ships were plying south through the Solomon Sea, heading for the Huon Gulf and the Port of Lae, only fifty air miles away.

Within moments, the convoy's location reached Port Moresby: 148 degrees east, 6.2 degrees south. By 1345, only fifteen minutes after the sighting, the crews of the 90th and 89th Squadrons were again scrambling into their B-25's. The skip bombs were still in their bomb-bays. The aircraft had been pre-flighted.

As they had this morning, the B-25's, in pairs, raced down the Dobodura Airstrip and hoisted themselves skyward. Spectators had again crowded the air field, for they had guessed that the convoy had been resighted or the bombers would not be taking off. And when the B-25's had disappeared into the northern horizon, the A-20's, also in pairs, roared down the same airstrip and hoisted themselves into the dense clouds. Colonel Bob Strickland once more watched from the control tower as the 3rd Group bombers disappeared.

Meanwhile, as soon as the P-40's found the Lae Resupply

Convoy, Japanese radiomen in the armada called Lae. "The enemy search planes have rediscovered us. Send interceptors to prevent any attack."

The 7th Fighter Division at Lae acknowledged the request. But the Japanese service troops did not hurry unnecessarily. After all, the convoy had just been spotted and at least an hour would pass before enemy bombers could reach the convoy. Besides, there was no point in hanging idly over the convoy and wasting precious fuel. So the Japanese ground crews worked steadily on the four squadrons of Zeros, 96 planes, that would escort the convoy into Lae.

However, only fifteen minutes after the convoy sighting, at 1345 hours, twelve B-25's of the 38th Bomb Group and twenty light bombers of the Australian 9th Operational Group suddenly zoomed in at low level over Lae Harbor, their bellies loaded with frag clusters and napalms. The abrupt arrival of low-level enemy planes completely surprised the Lae garrison. Not a man was in his antiaircraft gunpit and not a single fighter plane was in the air to meet the aerial invaders.

The attack was swift and devastating. Within ten minutes the Allied bombers had wreaked havoc on the Lae airstrips and their aircraft. They rendered the runways completely unserviceable as dozens of 30-pound bomb clusters left gaping holes in the airstrips. The same Allied striking force dropped more frag and napalm bombs on the exposed enemy fighter planes, sitting wing tip to wing tip on the taxi areas. At least half of the enemy fighter planes were destroyed; most of the rest were damaged. The few that escaped the holocaust would never take off. Service crews would need at least two or three hours to repair the Lae airstrips.

Meanwhile, the 3rd Group had begun its flight over the Solomon Sea. By the time the 38th and 9th had left their Lae target, the P-38 fighter plane escorts of the 49th Fighter Group had caught up to the skip bombers over the Solomon Sea. Soon, the fighters and bombers joined up as they streaked northwest towards the Huon Peninsula. They would meet no enemy interceptors when they reached the massive convoy an hour later.

AT 1430, MAJOR ED LARNER ALERTED the crews of his eleven B-25's and fifteen A-20's. "Alpine Leader to all units.

Ten minutes from target. Repeat: ten minutes from target. Stay alert. When we scramble, pick your targets in pairs. 3rd flight of the 90th and 4th flight of the 89th will attack as one unit. (These flights were abbreviated three-plane flights, instead of the normal four-plane flight.)

Sal Dineo hardly listened in the cockpit of Larner's B-25. He peered intensely outward, waiting to see the shapes on the sea, the convoy. But he heard the target before he saw it. A dull thunder boomed from the horizon. Then the copilot jerked as a sudden puff of black exploded some twenty-five yards from the cabin and rocked the lead B-25 of the 90th Squadron.

The copilot stretched his neck to look upwards but saw only the dull gray clouds. He had forgotten about the P-38 escorts who were far atop the nimbus depths. Morrissey and his fighter pilots would simply hover above to challenge any enemy interceptors they might find. Only if Larner called for them, would the Lightnings zoom down to join the bombers.

And from his bubble, Sergeant Joe Cardis again bit his lips as three more puffs of ack-ack followed the first. The sporadic barrages had stirred the lines of aircraft: wings tilted, noses dropped, or tails swayed. Cardis still saw nothing but the open sea under him. But if ack-ack bursts were already breaking around the bombers, what could they expect when the B-25's reached target?

Only a few minutes ahead of them, even as the pom-poms and five-inch guns thundered across the Solomon Sea, the Japanese convoy scattered. Four destroyers and the surviving cruiser shot forward full ahead, thick smoke streaming from their stacks, blending with the overcast. The prows of the ships sliced huge crests and sprayed white foam over the white-capped sea. Merchant vessels in the convoy wheeled to port or starboard, plying in a dozen different directions. By the time the first dots of B-25's loomed from the misty east, the convoy had spread itself over a five-mile square of the Solomon Sea.

Admiral Kimura and Captain Tishayuna stood on the bridge of the *Shirayuki* and peered through field glasses at the approaching aircraft.

"They appear much larger than attack planes," Captain Tishayuna said.

"Do they not sound like the medium bomber?" Kimura

asked his executive officer standing beside him.

"Yes," Tishayuna answered as the shapes became clearer. "They are indeed the B-25 medium bomber."

"Surely, they cannot attack from such a low altitude," Kimura said, half to himself. He looked above him at the dense clouds that almost touched the tall pagoda mast of his *Shirayuki.* "What do they plan? To strafe would simply be useless, and they would not be so foolish as to attack with fragmentation clusters."

"Perhaps torpedoes, Honorable Kimura."

Kimura's eyes brightened. "Ah, yes, Captain, they now use the medium bomber in an attempt to deliver a heavier torpedo attack. Notify all vessels to prepare for torpedoes."

"Yes, Admiral," Tishayuna answered before relaying Kimura's instructions to the wheelhouse.

With sailors at battle stations, the whoop alarms among the nineteen ships had ended. But gun crews increased their pom-pom and five-inch gunfire. The b-blooms of a hundred recoiling barrels shuddered the sea under them and shook the thick clouds above them.

Kimura never wavered from the bridge of the flag cruiser, but as the approaching Mitchells came closer to the scattered convoy, he said to Tishayuna: "Are all helmsmen prepared for torpedo attack?"

"Yes, Admiral."

And with the skip bombers, Major Ed Larner yelled into his radio. "Flak getting heavy and hot. Level off at 25 feet, just above the surface. When we scramble, pick your targets in pairs. And remember—fifteen seconds apart; stay fifteen seconds apart."

The approaching bombers fell almost to the sea, leveling off within prop range of the choppy water. The extremely low approach drew frowns from both Admiral Kimura and Captain Tishayuna. Kimura's mind whirled in confusion. What were these bombers doing? Torpedo attacks at such a low height might be as damaging to the attackers as to their targets. Surely, the Mitchells were not planning suicide missions—slam into the ships with loaded bomb bays. No, Kimura told himself, the Americans would not do that.

And even as the Japanese commander pondered the bombers' strategy, he noticed a disturbing fact. The gunners in the turret pits of his ships were firing furiously at the bombers without results. The sea-hugging Mitchells skimmed too low for the anti-aircraft guns. The pom-pom bursts were exploding above the oncoming aircraft. The five-inch guns, worse, were lobbing their flack shells even higher. Gunners frantically adjusted trajectory points—but to no avail. The bombers roared *below* the gunpit lines. The Japanese could not even bring barrels to 90 degree horizontal, let alone downward.

No elated looks sparkled from the Japanese gunners now; no confidence flashed from their eyes; no playful jostling ensued among the crews. They sat grim faced and tense, growing more frustrated in their futile attempt to hit the low-level aircraft. Desperately, gunnery officers called for small-caliber machine guns in an attempt to hit the oncoming bombers.

As the Mitchells roared into the enemy convoy, Larner cried into his radio. "Okay, boys, scramble! Wing, follow me in! We're going after that destroyer!"

Lt. Sal Dineo stared wide-eyed as the major dipped *Spook* towards the *Asashio*, the vanguard of the warships plying towards the American planes. Soon, the copilot could almost see the recoiling movements of the pom-pom guns and the exploding puffs above him. His body froze. If an ack-ack burst came low enough, they'd be blown to eternity.

Larner raced the Mitchell on, twenty-five feet above the surface of the sea. The major's face had again hardened. He squeezed his lips and ran his tongue around them. Then, when the plane came within four hundred yards of the destroyer, well beyond the range of the ship's machine guns, Larner pressed the buttons of his strafing guns. The sudden stream of tracers from eight 50-caliber nose guns raked the foredeck of the vessel like a spray of hot fire hoses. The blistering shots scattered the ship's defenders.

"What do they do? What do they do?" the executive officer anxiously asked the *Asashio's* commander.

"Perhaps unleash torpedoes at minimum range."

"Already, they are too near; they could not escape the explosions from their own torpedoes."

"Either that or they intend to smash into us." The commander of the *Asashio* yelled into his JV phone. "To port! To port!" The sleek destroyer veered in a 90-degree turn, the bow slapping across the whitecapped sea.

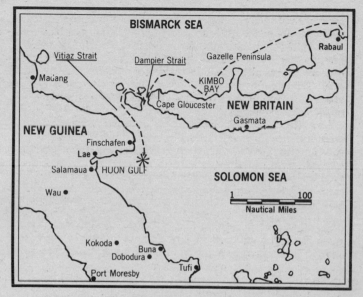

Map 6: Three hours out of Lae, the convoy is hit by skip bombers.

Larner grinned. The destroyer had reacted precisely as Pappy Gunn predicted. The veering ship had exposed its starboard beam. Larner brought the Mitchell just behind the bow of the destroyer. Within twenty-five yards, he unleashed two skip bombs and then yanked the stick of his plane. The B-25 leaped upwards just as the bombs pummelled into the waterline of the ship. When the Mitchell had safely cleared the vessel by more than two hundred yards, two staccato explosions opened the starboard gunwale in a pall of black concussions.

From his turret, Sergeant Joe Cardis, awestricken for a moment, finally pressed the triggers of his machine gun, spraying the port side of the destroyer as the Mitchell veered away. Japanese sailors scattered in panic. And even as the vessel listed to starboard, Larner's wingman drove his B-25 towards the stricken ship's starboard. Like the major, this pilot waited until he came within twenty-five yards before unleashing his skip bombs. The second Mitchell also cleared the mast of the destroyer and roared to a safe 200-yard distance before the second pair of explosions shook the sleek destroyer. Now, the smoke rose in a full wall of black along the entire starboard of the *Asashio*.

A terrible fear gripped the shocked Japanese sailors. The attacking bombers had come in like swooping, olive-drab eagles, clawing the warship with vicious strokes. The sailors pawed along the bulkheads, or staggered along the decks, or crawled to the nearest shelter. But in vain. By the time the wingman had joined Larner and the two planes had curled around to survey the damage, the ship had tilted to more than 30 degrees.

"Let's finish her off," Larner called to his wingman.

The two B-25's again roared into the destroyer's starboard side. Half of the four released skip bombs from this second run opened two more huge gaps in the warship's waterline. The twin Mitchell hits, at least six 500-pound skip bombs, had opened the entire starboard side of the hull. In a nightmarish moment, two planes had sent tons of water into the holds of the destroyer like a rampaging flood. Hundreds of Japanese sailors, bewildered and stunned, scrambled in panic over the sides or simply hurled themselves into the sea. Reason disrupted, they ignored the frantic calls of superiors to launch lifeboats or rafts.

Within five minutes, the *Asashio* capsized and began the slow plunge to the bottom of the Solomon Sea. Cardis stared in amazement at the sudden, devastating effect of the skip bomb. He also stared at the countless heads bobbing on the sea. Besides the Asashio's crew complement, three hundred rescued soldiers from the transport sunk yesterday were aboard the destroyer.

IN OTHER PARTS OF THE SOLOMON SEA, the slaughter continued. Captain Don McNutt of the 90th Squadron's abbreviated three-plane 4th Flight, led his attackers at the surviving tanker, despite the frantic crossfire of two destroyers. The heavily laden merchant ship flopped about the sea like a harpooned whale, trying desperately to avoid the trio of Mitchells.

But, after two runs, the helpless tanker had been struck by several waterline skip bombs. The tanker exploded in a huge ball of fire and thick smoke. The bulky vessel nearly leaped out of the water in a dying explosion and then flopped back into the sea. She disappeared quickly, with all hands, under the choppy Soloman Sea. There would be no need for secondary strafing runs.

Even as the two accompanying destroyers fired frantically after Captain McNutt's three-plane flight, other duos of B-25's leveled off towards one of the warships, the destroyer *Hatsuyuki*. The commander of the vessel had barely lurched the ship to port when the first two B-25's unleashed their skip bombs on the port bow. Before the crew could stave off the angry sea pouring into the fore compartments, a second duo of Mitchells unleashed four more skip bombs on the starboard bow. Two sailed high and hit the superstructure, but the others hit the foreward waterline. The bow of the destroyer plunged under the choppy sea like a startled submarine under attack.

As the ship's crew abandoned ship, the first duo of B-25's arched back and slammed three out of four skip bombs on the port and starboard bows. The aft of the ship rose out of the water like the head of a serpent and splashed on the surface of the water. Then, the fatally wounded *Hatsuyuki* plunged to the bottom of the sea.

Now came the first four A-20's of Major Glen Clark's 89th Squadron. The quartet of planes did not fail to score. The aircraft stormed into the wounded transport, the one injured yesterday by the 38th Bomb Group. Japanese sailors and soldiers, stricken with terror, watched the planes skim into them like the twin arms of death. The first two A-20's skidded their bombs just behind the port bow. Fifteen seconds later, the second A-20 unleashed two skip bombs on the same side amidship.

Fire and flood crews never had a chance. Before they could even reach the gush of sea water roaring into the gaps, the A-20's returned for their second run. Four more skip bombs tore into the *maru*'s hull. The sea poured into the holds like an unleashed flood: swiftly, the heavily loaded troop carrier gurgled under the choppy surface of the Solomon Sea.

Aboard the *Shirayuki*, the faces of Admiral Kimura and Captain Tishayuna had paled to a concrete white. Fifteen planes had scored 34 horrifying hits. Within minutes, they had sent two warships and two merchant ships to the bottom of the Solomon Sea. Further, they had slain countless sailors and soldiers with strafing fire. Neither officer could even imagine such quick devastation from air attacks. They had recalled aircraft hitting ships with dozens of bombs, flattening superstructures, knocking out steering gear, engine rooms, gun turrets; but now, with some new type of delayed fuse bombs, little more than a dozen bombers had roared within touching distance of the sea and murdered the convoy.

"Where are the escorts, the escorts?" Kimura cried frantically.

"There has been a delay at Lae," Captain Tishayuna answered.

"I cannot believe what has happened; I cannot believe! We must stop this slaughter at all costs—at all costs!" Kimura screamed.

"They fly too low, Admiral. Our antiaircraft guns are ineffective."

Kimura gripped the railing of the *Shirayuki*'s bridge, squeezing his fists until the veins cracked blue lines on his skin. "Captain, radio Cape Gloucester, Gasmata, Madang. and Wewak. Tell them we must have escort if we are to survive."

"It has already been done," Tishayuna answered.

But even as the admiral and his executive officer waited in helpless horror, new flights of A-20's from the 89th Squadron came roaring into the battered convoy.

A sextet of A-20's descended on the *Nojima Maru*, the transport also damaged the previous day by B-17's. The flight leader, as he approached the vessel, called into his radio: "Remember, you guys, don't get cute. No pop shots at stacks or guns pits. Just drop those skip bombs on the waterline. I'll take port, amidship; you guys come in at the aft and bow. Tail flight, use the same pattern on the starboard side after we've made our run. We'll open up that ship like Swiss cheese and let the sea do the rest."

Moments later, a series of b-blooms by a trio of A-20's wracked the port side of the ship. The aircraft had unleashed their skip bombs within twenty-five yards of the waterline and zoomed upwards and away. Then came a second punch on starboard from three other A-20's. The big transport never had a chance. She settled quickly under the Solomon Sea, keel first.

As the attack by the remaining A-20's continued, two more ships of the once proud convoy began the descent to the bottom of the sea. The freighters *Kamo Maru* and *Shichisei Maru* fell victim to the last wave of A-20's and those B-25's that had not yet expended all bombs.

Finally, it was over. And the dull, gray day was markedly appropriate for the funeral in the Solomon Sea.

Chapter Twelve

PREPARING FOR THE KILL

The heavy cloud cover had failed the "Eel of the Pacific," for the Allies had been able to overcome the foul weather. Admiral Kimura's proud convoy lay foundering in the Solomon Sea, a mere 50 knots from Lae, a destination that now seemed an ocean's length away. Only twelve of the Lae Resupply Convoy's 22 ships that had set sail from Rabaul on the night of February 28 were still afloat, and many of these surviving ships were damaged. Somehow, neither Kimura nor his sailors could fathom the horrifying reality that two dozen light bombers could sink seven ships in a matter of minutes.

It is true that General Whitehead had acted wisely when he ordered the air attack on the Lae airfields as soon as his reconnaissance planes had sighted the convoy. It is also true that Whitehead had used good judgment in allowing Colonel Bob Strickland to refit his 3rd Group bombers with skip bombs after conventional tactics had failed, especially with the foul weather. But in alerting only their fighter planes at Lae, the Japanese command had followed the same faulty line of thinking that had worked against them during earlier engagements in the Pacific war.

The Imperial Japanese Staff had always been too cautious, even when they possessed far superior numbers. They were never willing to commit more troops or planes or ships than necessary, especially in air and sea battles.

At Pearl Harbor, the Japanese had come up short of a true knockout blow because they were too cautious to move in for the kill and perhaps occupy the Hawaiian Islands. In the Battle of the Coral Sea, though their forces far outnumbered the understrength Allies, they retired after suffering the loss of a single carrier, even though they had sunk two American carriers. In the Battle of Midway, although Japan's air and sea units had suffered losses, they still had a formidable, unscathed striking force in the area; but instead of pressing on against the depleted American carrier force, they again retired.

The same might be said of the Solomons campaign. Japanese caution was the major reason for American success at Guadalcanal. In most of the naval fights during the Solomon campaign, the Japanese task forces did more damage to the American navy than the Americans had meted out. Yet, after successful naval engagements, such as the Battles of Savo Island or Cape Esperance, the Japanese naval units retired after their victories instead of pressing forward. As a result, they had allowed the American navy to lick its wounds and regain its strength.

As to Japan's aerial strategy, the worst kind of caution prevailed. While American pilots were generally superior to Japanese pilots, and while the American P-38 was superior to the Hamp and Zero fighter plane, the Japanese could muster many more planes. Further, they were superior to the earlier P-39 and P-40 used by the American air force prior to 1943. Yet they never sent more than a squadron or two of fighter planes into an aerial engagement. They thus allowed even terms to inferior numbers of Allied army and navy units, which could rarely muster more than a squadron or two of planes to meet a Japanese challenge. So, because of the superior training of Allied airmen, the Allied pilots usually defeated their opponents.

The Japanese also followed this caution in the use of their bombers. Hundreds of Sally and Betty bombers sat on the many Japanese air bases in the Bismarck Archipelago, especially at Rabaul. Yet they rarely committed more than 20 or 30 bombers to an air attack against an Allied base. Against navy ships, the Japanese only used their light naval fighter-bombers. They rarely sent their heavy and medium bombers that were only a stone's throw from the Ironbottom Strait in the Solomons where most of the action took place during the Guadalcanal operation. The biggest raid ever conducted by the Japanese in the Southwest Pacific was the 50-plane raid on Port Moresby in February, 1942.

At the conference in Rabaul in February 1943, where the Japanese staff planned operation 157, Admiral Junichi Kasaka of the Imperial Eleventh Naval Air Fleet, boasted of his great airpower. He could count hundreds of planes scattered among the various Japanese airfields in the Bismarck Archipelago. Why then, didn't Admiral Kasaka maintain a cover of a hundred or even two-hundred planes over the convoy all the way from Rabaul to the Huon Gulf? Kasaka's land-based aircraft were never more than an hour or two from the route of Kimura's convoy. And, ironically, Kasaka did maintain heavy air cover over the convoy during the early part of the voyage, when the convoy was far into the Bismarck Sea and out of range of Allied medium or light bombers. But he failed to maintain this cover as the convoy neared Huon Gulf, within range of any Allied plane in New Guinea.

Moreover, Admiral Gunichi Mikawa, commander of the Eighth Outer Sea Fleet, could proclaim that he had all but chased the American navy from the Bismarck Archipelago because of his superior numbers in naval ships. Why then, didn't he allot one or even two aircraft carriers to escort the hugely important 22-ship convoy into Lae? Again, because the Japanese had an obsession with safeguarding their heavy strength. They kept planes and ships ever in reserve for future emergency.

This hesitant commitment of forces in any action against the Allies, this lack of aggression, and the squeamish reaction to battle losses, ultimately destroyed Japan's hopes for conquest. The destruction on the Solomon Sea on the afternoon of 3 March 1943 illustrated the folly of this obsession with excess caution. A mere 26 medium and light bombers, with only 16 escorting fighter planes had enjoyed a field day against the Lae Resupply Convoy. Admiral Kasaka could have easily hung a couple hundred fighter planes above the convoy at all times. Had they been over the Solomon Sea, the 3rd Group bombers may not have come within sighting range of the convoy much less skip bombing range.

Despite the superiority of the P-38 and the superiority of American pilots, Colonel Bob Morrissey's 16-fighter plane escort could not have protected 26 bombers against hundreds of Japanese fighter planes. Sheer numbers alone could have overwhelmed the attacking American aircraft. Instead, the Japanese had foolishly allowed the Lae Resupply Convoy to sail unprotected. And worse, they had left Lae unprotected so that a small number of planes from the 38th and 9th Groups, without fighter escort, could destroy the air fields.

Perhaps the Japanese had naively assumed that Kimura had fooled the Allies as to his location. Perhaps they assumed that he would reach Lae without further harassment. They should have considered, of course, that Allied reconn planes would be operating around the clock to rediscover the convoy. And, unfortunately for Admiral Kimura, the hour of the skip bomb attack had been one of those hours in which no Japanese escort planes had been protecting the armada.

Because of the Japanese fanaticism with maintaining heavy reserves, Imamura's staff in Rabaul had forced Admiral Kimura to use whatever ruses he could, including gambling on continued foul weather, to avoid Allied air attacks. Kimura could depend with certainty only on the skill of his helmsmen and on his own shipboard antiaircraft gunners, who had performed admirably until they met the unexpected skip bombers.

Conversely, the Allied general staff rarely considered keeping strength in reserve. They seldom had any early in the war, anyway. The Allies normally went for broke. General Whitehead had never once considered the idea of holding aircraft in reserve. He scratched and poked to ready every serviceable bomber and fighter plane he could find, cleaning out his air bases of Dobodura, Port Moresby, and Tufi. He sent anything that could fly after the Japanese convoy; and no Fifth Air Force staff member ever questioned this strategy.

NOW, THANKS TO JAPANESE overcautiousness and Allied aggressiveness, the excited mood among Allied troops in the Southwest Pacific contrasted sharply with the somber mood of Japanese troops.

In the dozen or so military camps and bases in Allied Papua, men responded with awe to the news from the Solomon Sea. At the Australian base in Wau, the Kanga Force listened with gaping mouths and astonished faces. Each new sinking report had heightened the silence. Only their minds had whirred in that constant hope for a miracle.

At Dobodura, the control tower technicians had set up a PA system so the listening hundreds around the airstrips could hear the monitored radio reports: "Right on the nose!" or "Follow us in for strafing!" or "We got 'em, boys!" or "Just drop the bombs on the waterline!"

Like those at Wau, these men at Dobodura also sat motionless and silent under the dense, racing overcast—trying to believe and comprehend the stunning reports coming from the Solomon Sea.

In the control tower itself, Pappy Gunn chomped a little harder on his cigar with each new score on the Lae Resupply Convoy. Colonel Bob Strickland merely pursed his lips. Neither man spoke. It was like the superstitious taboo of not commenting during a potential no-hit baseball game.

Inside the old hotel at Port Moresby, activity had ground to a standstill. No papers rustled, no typewriters clacked, no footsteps thudded across the warped floors. Men sat or stood. But they listened. And here, too, technicians had installed a PA unit on the wraparound porch to accommodate the dozens of curious men gathered on the weeded grounds in front of the hotel. Diggers, sailors, dogfaces, airmen all listened intently. Yesterday, fifty-three planes had only sunk three ships and lost three aircraft. It was almost beyond their comprehension that 26 planes had sunk seven vessels, damaged more, and had not lost a single bomber. Further, Colonel Morrissey's 49th Fighter Group had not run into a single Japanese interceptor and the listening Allied soldiers could only speculate as to why.

But no such elation reverberated through the bases of the Japanese in the Bismarck Archipelago. General Toru Okabe and his staff in Eighteenth Army Headquarters at Lae listened in horror to the frantic pleas from Admiral Kimura, and Okabe could only wonder whether or not General Hatazo Adachi himself was among the casualties.

In other parts of Lae, the revelry of an earlier hour had faded to a stunned silence. The *sake* bottles lay untouched, half empty. The soldiers sat in dazed apprehension. The work on the landing jetties and launch boats had ceased.

And across the Solomon Sea, at Rabaul, General Hitoshi Imamura and his staff also sat in disbelief. They too wondered if their combat commanders—Kimura, Adachi, or Nakano—had perished with hundreds of other casualties in this vicious Allied attack.

But strategists in war have little time to mope or celebrate. The Japanese still had a formidable armada floating on the Solomon Sea. Both sides knew it. With Larner's cry to go home, new orders had to be issued.

General Whitehead spoke to two staff colonels. "How far are those ships from Lae?"

"Maybe three or four hours."

"Enough time for the 3rd Group to get back there again?"

The two colonels looked at each other in surprise before one of them spoke again. "You don't intend to send them back again?"

"There's still a dozen ships floating out there."

"But General, every Jap fighter plane in the Southwest Pacific will be over that convoy within the next hour. The 3rd had the surprise element. The Japanese apparently did not expect the strike, and certainly not with fuse bombs. We fooled them once, but can we do it twice?"

General Whitehead leaned over his desk and glowered. "I want every fighter plane in Papua ready for escort, even photo planes if we can load 'em with guns."

"Yes sir."

Again, Whitehead was acting as most Allied commanders in the Southwest Pacific—shoot the works. And even as the 90th and 89th Squadrons meshed for the trip back to Dobodura, not a plane lost, Pappy Gunn wasted no time. He called the Dobodura airdrome OD officer as soon as he heard from General Whitehead. "We just got word from the general," Gunn told the OD officer. "Have your trucks on the strip and ready. As soon as Larner and Morrissey touch down, you're to reload for another takeoff. You're to chase those returning planes right down the runways if you have to. They're to take off as soon as you can reload and refuel them."

Then Pappy Gunn told the tower officer to put the airstrip off limits to all aircraft except those from the returning 3rd and 49th Groups. Nothing must interfere with a quick landing since the two groups would refuel and reload for a second strike. The control tower should direct all transports, reconnaissance planes, or any other aircraft to other airfields, such as Tufi or Port Moresby. And all nonessential personnel were ordered to clear the area.

Next, Pappy Gunn made three phone calls: to the 49th and 35th Fighter Groups in Dobodura and to the 9th Australian Operational Group at Tufi. How many fighter planes could they load and rendezvous in one hour? The deputy commander of the 49th had sixteen P-40's in the revetment areas, but the group's sixteen P-38's were out on escort with the 3rd Group. The P-40's could be readied immediately. Colonel Richard Legg of the 35th Fighter Group, after a quick survey, said he could mount fifteen P-38's and fifteen P-39 Airacobras. The RAAF commander of the Australian 9th at Tufi said he could supply sixteen P-40's from the 75th and 77th Squadrons and about a dozen Beaufighters from their 30th Squadron. The P-40's were in Wau after their recent reconnaissance duty.

Pappy Gunn then told the officers of all three air groups to ready their pursuit planes within an hour and await instructions for their escort duty rendezvous point. The personnel of the 35th, 49th, and 9th responded at once, with both ground crews and fighter pilots racing to get ready. They had heard the uncanny Solomon Sea reports and they relished the opportunity to participate in a second assault against the convoy, even though a sky full of Hamps and Zeros might be waiting for them the second time around.

After Gunn had readied the fighter plane units, he called Major Ed Larner and Colonel Bob Morrissey through the Dobodura control tower. "This is ADVON High Point; ADVON High Point to Alpine and White Leaders."

"What's up, Pappy?" Ed Larner responded.

"You and white Leader are going out again—just as soon as you can reload and gulp a cup of coffee."

"You're crazy!" Larner huffed over his radio.

"Larner," the authoritative voice of General Whitehead

suddenly barked over the High Point radio band, "get your ass back to Dobo on the double! You and Gunn drove me crazy with that skip bomb thing and you knocked out half the convoy with it. Like it or not, you and your people are carrying the ball. No matter how you slice it, it's your show. Pappy's already got armament and gas trucks ready to reload you. Get your ass home!"

"Yes sir, General," Larner grinned. "We'll come in with our bomb bays open. Those ordnance guys'll only have to shove more skip bombs in our bays and some benzedrine in our blood."

WHILE THE 49TH FIGHTER GROUP and 3rd Bomb Group hurried back to Dobodura, the Japanese also moved. Even before the last numbing report from the Solomon Sea had reached Rabaul, General Hitoshi Imamura had summoned his staff to his headquarters. And before the last A-20 had left the foundering Lae Resupply Convoy, Admiral Jinichi Kasaka, Admiral Gunichi Mikawa, and other staff members had assembled in Imamura's bungalow.

The Eighth Area commander glowered first at Mikawa. Why hadn't Mikawa, with his countless warships, given Kimura more protection? Why, in fact, had the Imperial Navy not even offered a carrier for the convoy? Mikawa did not answer, for he knew that Imamura was questioning his own judgment as well as that of Admiral Mikawa. True indeed, why hadn't they offered Kimura more warship protection?

Imamura next glowered at Admiral Kasaka. The air chief commanded some 400 serviceable aircraft in his Eleventh Air Fleet. Weren't the airfields at Wewak, Madang, Wewak, Gasmata, Cape Gloucester, and Lae crammed with aircraft? And wasn't Rabaul itself also crammed with planes? Yet, a mere squadron or two had only intermittently hung over the convoy, and none had been over the armada at the time of the most devastating attack. Why were only the fighter planes at Lae on alert? Why not the fighter units in the other Japanese air bases of the Bismarck Archipelago?

Once again, however, Imamura was questioning his own judgment as well as that of his air chief.

But half a loaf was better than none. Twelve ships were still plying towards Lae. Foul weather still hung over the

Bismarck Archipelago to rule out the use of conventional bombers against the convoy. The Allies could only return with their skip bombs. Their crews would be tired and they would need at least two hours to return to the convoy. Could Kasaka prevent a second numbing blow, perhaps a fatal one?

"I have already directed the use of every available interceptor plane to protect Admiral Kimura," Kasaka answered General Imamura. "We will construct so great a defensive screen that no bomber force will reach the honorable Kimura. Even now, our Mitsubishi I's and Mitsubishi II's have left Cape Gloucester to hover over the convoy, while other Eleventh Air Fleet escort planes at Gasmata will soon be there. And," he gestured, "I have spoken with Colonel Hato Shinohara who leads our Seventh Fighter Division in New Guinea. He has assured me that every aircraft in Madang and Wewak will strike out towards the Solomon Sea. He further promised me that our aircraft will attack any approaching planes as locust attacks a wheat field. We shall overwhelm any new Allied attack. We shall have a shield of planes as thick as the clouds above the sea."

Perhaps a sudden shock is the best way to shake one from routine habit. The shock of the skip bomb attack in the Solomon Sea this afternoon may have indeed rattled Kasaka from his traditional sense of caution, a characteristic of all Japanese commanders. Kasaka had apparently decided to go for broke, too.

"How many aircraft can we muster?" Imamura asked.

"At a minimum, 200. Be assured, General, Admiral Kimura will reach Lae with the remainder of the convoy."

"Good, good," Imamura sighed.

On the Solomon Sea, Admiral Kimura had shaken himself from his numbed trance and was regrouping his mauled convoy to continue towards Lae. The six surviving destroyers along with the cruiser had whirled about the sea picking up survivors. Within a half hour, they had plucked more than 1600 soldiers and sailors from the murky waters.

Three of the transports were still intact—half the 77th Brigade and more than a regiment of the 51st Division. From the sea, warships had salvaged at least another regiment. Those saved from the *Nojima Maru* had been placed aboard the crowded *Teiyo Maru* of Captain Matsumoto and the other two transports. The others remained aboard the rescuing cruiser and destroyers. Thus, Kimura still had over 7,000 combat troops.

Two freighters, completely undamaged, still carried their full loads of of equipment and material—nearly two thirds of the supplies loaded at Rabaul: tons of munitions, guns, food, and vehicles would reach Lae. Kimura had lost his tankers, but submarines could always bring in fuel.

The worst had been the loss of the cruiser and two destroyers, but many of the sailors had been saved.

And now, two squadrons of Zeros from Cape Gloucester whirred over the zig-zagging ships. And soon, two squadrons of Hamps hovered above the clouds. The aircraft—96 planes—would be the first in a swarm of cover promised by General Kasaka. More planes were on their way from Wewak.

So, all things considered, Kimura was satisfied.

By 1515, forty-five minutes after the skip bomb attack, the Japanese had regrouped twelve vessels, though some of them were badly damaged and one was taken into tow by a destroyer. Once more, Kimura plodded forward with his convoy on a two-four-six course. He soon entered Huon Gulf, three short hours away from his destination at Lae.

When Kimura looked up at the Zeros, Captain Tishayuna stood next to the admiral. "They are but a fraction of the escort that will protect us. As these Mitsubishi I's stay with us under the low cloud cover, so will another sixty Mitsubishi II's remain above the clouds to discourage another Yankee attack. And still another hundred aircraft will arrive from Wewak, Madang, and Gasmata."

Kimura only nodded.

"But more than this," the executive officer continued. "A squadron of Mitsibushi I's will patrol the skies to the east. Not only will they provide ample warning should the Americans attempt to attack us again, but they will represent the first line of defense against any such attack."

Kimura nodded again and then watched the Zero fighters dart and arch around the Lae Resupply Convoy like frolicking wrens.

BUT SO, TOO, HAD THE ALLIES readied their aircraft. By 1600, Allied fighter planes had also stirred. The 77th and 75th RAAF P-40 squadrons had taken off from Tufi. Both the P-39's and P-38's of the 35th Fighter Group were already airborne and circling restlessly over the Solomon Sea, waiting for the bombers. The P-40's of the 49th Group were also waiting over the Solomon Sea. And, as ground crews feverishly refueled and reloaded the 3rd Group bombers, the ground crews of the 49th Fighter Group were refueling and reloading their P-38's.

Every hand at Dobodura had offered to help the ordnance men in their frantic effort to refill gas tanks, bomb bays, and strafing guns of both the bombers and fighters. Within thirty minutes all available Allied fighters, ninety of them, would be ready for the renewed attack, this time in the Huon Gulf. The thirty-one P-38 Lightnings of the 35th and 49th Groups would act as high cover, since the P-38's were more than a match for Zero or Hamp fighters at high altitudes. The Warhawk P-40's would fly at low level, to meet any interceptors under the clouds before the interceptors could reach the skip bombers behind them. The Beaufighters and P-39's would chain the bombers.

The 90th Squadron's B-25's and the 89th Squadron's A-20's, at the moment, represented the greatest threat to the Japanese since the fight in the Southwest Pacific began. None of the other Allied bomber crews had been trained in the skip bomb technique. So Fifth Air Force was sparing no effort to protect these skip bombers and their crews.

At 1630 the eleven Mitchells, reloaded with skip bombs, zoomed once more in pairs down the Dobodura bomber strip. Right behind them came the fifteen reloaded A-20's. Spectators in vehicles around the runways felt a renewed doubt. They knew the Japanese would not be caught off guard twice. They wondered if the spunky 3rd Bomb Group crews, with their limited fighter cover, would even reach the Huon Gulf.

And in fact the Japanese were indeed waiting for them with 200 fighter planes. The Japanese, like the Allies, had appeared to have thrown caution to the wind. They now appeared willing to strip their air bases of most of their fighter planes. General Rimpei Ota, commander of the 7th Air Division in New Guinea, had totally concurred with Jinichi Kasaka. They would spare nothing and they would place in command Colonel Hato Shinohara, a Japanese air ace against American fighter pilots. Ota agreed with Kasaka that Shinohara would inspire the fighter pilots of the 7th Fighter Division to make every effort against Allied attack planes.

Shinohara eagerly accepted the task. "They will not reach the honorable Kimura again," Colonel Shinohara promised Kasaka.

Shinohara had already completed his strategy. Two squadrons of Zeros, 48 planes, would hang at sea level around the convoy. Another squadron, 24 planes, would reconnoiter east of the convoy as a first line of defense. Forty-eight Hamps would loiter above the clouds, waiting for the opportunity to zoom downward out of the billowy mists to hit the bombers from above. Finally, another six squadrons of fighter planes remained on the ready in Madang and Gasmata. Altogether, 260 fighter planes would defend the battered Lae Resupply Convoy against a second skip bomb attack.

Both sides, therefore, were going all out in the Huon Gulf. Within the next hour, the greatest aerial dogfight of the Southwest Pacific war would rattle and squeal over Huon Gulf. On the Allied fighter planes depended the success or failure of the 26 bombers.

The question: Could 90 Allied fighter planes, many of which had already put in a day's work along with their pilots, be a match for 200 adversaries? Numerically, the answer was' an obvious no. But, despite all urgings to the contrary, would the Japanese squadron leaders operate in their traditional habit of caution, committing their aircraft in piecemeal fashion? Or could the esteemed Colonel Hato Shinohara inspire the pilots to fight as one mass of locusts?

Chapter Thirteen

FLIGHT THROUGH HELL

The mile-thick clouds swirled in distorted wads and shapes, thickening, spreading, meshing, changing from gray to black, back to white, and reverting to gray again. They whirled in rolling puffs or glided in dense globs. They mushroomed upwards towards the sky or billowed downward to touch the water.

Colonel Bob Morrissey steered a tight parade of P-38's in a line of V's at 10,000 feet above the clouds at the relatively slow speed of 300 knots. Six other Lightnings, scouts, raced forward and then darted back in sweeping arches to the main upstairs fighter formations. As the high escorts from the 49th and 39th American Fighter Groups whined closer to Huon Gulf, the scooting fighters lessened their outward prods and remained within sight of Morrissey's lead P-38.

The P-38 high cover under the command of Colonel Bob Morrissey was designated White Leader.

Below the clouds, less than a hundred feet above the choppy sea, soared another mass of escorts. The 49th Fighter Group's P-40's and the seventeen P-40's of the 9th Australian

Operational Group also zoomed westward in formation. The 32 Warhawks also droned in a line of tight V formations. Another half dozen P-40's shot forward over the sea like searching gulls or darted back to the main formations. These low scouts, too, shortened their outward patrols as the Warhawks neared the target plying towards Lae.

The low escort, under the command of Major Bill Martin of the 49th Fighter Group, had been designated Gray Leader.

Finally, in huddled diamonds behind the P-40's, came the B-25's and A-20's, skimming over the crest of the Solomon Sea. The crews of the 26 bombers sat mutely in the cabins or bubble turrets, with only the voice of Major Ed Larner, the commander designated Alpine Leader, breaking the silence.

"This is Alpine Leader. All gunners stay alert. Stay Alert. Report any signs of enemy aircraft."

Next to Larner, Lieutenant Sal Dineo stared at the gloom beyond his cabin window, the drab gray afternoon light between the dark heavy clouds and the blackish blue sea. Apprehensively, he waited for the sudden pounce of enemy fighters from the west.

Then a call from Major Bill Martin. "This is Gray Leader to Alpine. Estimate target at forty miles, forty miles."

Less than twenty minutes. Larner licked his lips and searched the gloom ahead of him. He saw only the outlines of escorting fighters in their geometric V's. He spoke into his radio to the 49th Fighter Group commander. "Alpine to White Leader . . . White Leader. Interceptors. What about interceptors?"

"Nothing yet, but don't worry. You'll have the Aussies along any minute."

The bombers trailed their P-40 escorts for another five minutes before a new arrival of aircraft whined through the 3rd Group diamonds like a swarm of bees. The twelve Beaufighters of the 9th Operational RAAF and the fifteen P-39's of the 35th American Fighter Group were taking up their positions around the bombers. Larner had barely begun to count them when the vanguard Warhawks shot forward like excited crows and disappeared. The newly arrived fighter escort tightened their ring around the bombers.

"Don't get shook up, Mate," the 75th Squadron Leader, Bill Archer, radioed Larner. "What our blokes up front don't stop, we'll give a bloody go back here."

"Like leeches, Leader, like leeches," Archer assured.

FROM HIS TURRET, SERGEANT CARDIS watched the Aeracobras and Beaufighters jell around them. He was following their weaving movements when the sound of 50-caliber guns suddenly reverberated with a deafening din. The gunner jerked in his seat. In the two hundred foot tunnel between the clouds and the sea, the gunfire echoed past him like the amplified roll of drums. Joe Cardis whirled in his turret and peered into the murkiness around him. He saw nothing, but he jerked again as the sudden whine of a plane nearby hurt his eardrum. In a gaping, momentary glance, he caught sight of a silver object and then saw a splashing explosion in the sea to his left. A Japanese Zero had become the first victim of an afternoon dog fight over the Huon Gulf.

But more important, the young gunner now knew that Japanese fighter planes would indeed be over the Huon Gulf to protect their target against any second incursion by the bombers.

"All gunners, stay alert!" Larner shouted into his radio. "Watch it up high! Up high!"

Cardis craned his neck and stared at the dense clouds overhead. He saw only the endless mass of misty gray and black racing past him. He stiffened again, however, when another reverberation of 50-caliber gunfire shocked his eardrums. And as before, he saw the death of a Zero. The silver plane, black smoke streaming from its fuselage skimmed towards the sea in an uncontrollable glide. It wavered up and down before it came to an abrupt, splashing end. By the time the downed enemy fighter plane exploded, Cardis felt the concussion. Then his B-25 moved far beyond the downed Japanese plane.

"Cardis, are you keeping a sharp watch?"

The gunner instinctively looked upwards and squinted into the clouds. "Yes sir," he answered Major Larner, "but I don't see anything."

"They're having a donnybrook up front. Stay ready for anything."

True. The vanguard P-40's, the low cover, were engaging Japanese fighter planes.

In the cockpit of *Spook*, Larner studied his instrument

dials, checked his bomb release buttons, and checked the firing buttons of his nose cannons. Then he looked about him. The Australian Beaufighters and American P-40's still flew in their weaving patterns. Interceptors had not yet reached the bombers.

Next to the pilot, Sal Dineo sat nervously, counting the minutes or occasionally glancing at the instrument dial. He tried to peer beyond the Warhawks far in front of him, looking for signs of the convoy. But he could see nothing except the endless gray waters of the Huon Gulf.

Suddenly the B-25 jerked, rattling Larner and Dineo. A tinkle of glass, the light clank of metal, and the split second whine of a diving plane deafened the two airmen. A woosh of air roared through the cabin.

"We got hit, Major!" Dineo cried.

"Emergency canopy," Larner cried. And as Dineo quickly turned in his seat and yanked the emergency pane of plexiglass across the broken glass, Larner shouted into his intercom. "Cardis! Are you asleep back there? We got hit. Didn't you see that bandit?"

"N—no sir," Cardis stammered.

"We're only minutes from target. We've got enough trouble so stay alert, you understand!"

"Y—Yes sir."

"How much damage, Sal?"

Dineo scanned the area behind his cabin seat. "Ripped a few holes in the first aid kit and dioxide hose. Doesn't look serious."

"Unless we get a fire in this cabin."

"We have an auxiliary hose, Major. Shall I put it on?"

"No time. That convoy'll be coming up any minute."

Cardis, meanwhile, with renewed alertness, moved his head constantly in a 180-degree arc, scanning the clouds over him. At fifty feet above the sea, nothing would come from underneath. And for a full minute he heard no more whines or chattering guns. The fight up front between the P-40's and Zekes had apparently abated.

Cardis nearly relaxed when the whine of aircraft suddenly burst again, this time from deep within the clouds. He stared up frantically, listening intently, but saw nothing. His nerves twisted in frustration, as though he was being pestered by unseen mosquitos inside the netting of a sleeping

cot. Then, abruptly, a silver shape broke out of the mist, its
guns chattering in angry bursts. By the time Cardis could
aim his own guns, the shape had zoomed past him and had
already disappeared into the overcast to his left. The gunner's heart pounded, but he saw no sign of damage on the B-
25.

However, he got another scolding from Larner. "Cardis,
what the hell happened? You didn't get off a shot!"

"S Sorry, sir. It happened too fast."

Another burst of 30-caliber fire shook the air. The tracers
ripped the top of the fuselage between the gunner's bubble
and tail. However, Cardis reacted quickly. As the Zero
streaked past *Spook*, the gunner whirled to 90 degrees and
sent a chattering burst of 50-caliber fire at the enemy plane.
The underbelly of the Japanese Zero fighter exploded in a
flat whoof, and a trail of black smoke gushed backwards into
the clouds. The enemy aircraft whined desperately, twisting
and turning, trying to rise into the clouds. But the Zero's
engine wound down to a sputtering cough. A few seconds
later it dropped into the sea. Cardis craned his neck to look,
but again the B-25 had left the crash sight. The gunner, disappointed, settled back in his seat.

"Now you're showing life," Larner suddenly spoke into the
intercom. "You got that one! Our tail flight confirmed the
Zeke burning and sinking."

"Yes sir," Cardis said.

A smile cut lines on the young gunner's sweat-stained
face. But, there was little time for self-congratulations.
Again, the grating squeal of enemy planes filtered through
the dense overcast. They were more high pitched this time,
the distinct sounds of Hamps. Cardis waited for them to
break out of the clouds. His eyes watered from staring so
hard. But he saw nothing. Instead, he suddenly heard the low
whines of P-38's join the high whines of Hamps and he
guessed that another clash had emerged high above the
clouds. His suspicions were confirmed when he heard the
abrupt echoes of 50- and 30-caliber machine guns. He prayed
that the upstairs P-38 fighter cover would not be driven from
the sky.

His hopes rose, when a moment later, he saw a Hamp
fighter fall out of the clouds to his left and tumble crazily until it plopped into the sea. Before the eddies from the crash

had settled, two more Hamps burst out of the overcast, swiftly and unexpectedly. Cardis whirled his guns but the enemy fighters were completely ignoring the long formation of bombers. Cardis saw why. One Hamp was engulfed in its own billowy smoke; the other had lost most of its tail. Both Hamps were desperately trying to right themselves, but neither succeeded. The two Japanese fighter planes plunged into the murky sea and the sinking aircraft faded into the distance.

Cardis felt a veneer of comfort. The P-38's were doing well. They were knocking the Hamps out of the sky and through the clouds just as the P-40's, the low cover, had been thwarting Zero fighters just above the surface of Huon Gulf.

HOWEVER, THE TASK IN THE BRIGHT BLUE SKY above the clouds was not as cut-and-dried as it appeared to Joe Cardis in his bubble turret. Far above the billowy clouds, Colonel Bob Morrissey and his P-38 pilots had already engaged two swarms of Japanese Hamps. The three victims that had fallen through the clouds were but a fraction of the planes that tried to break through the P-38 cover. And perhaps the P-38 pilots were tiring, for they were not as alert as they had been a few moments earlier.

"Wing, a Hamp at four o'clock high!" Morrissey yelled anxiously into his radio.

"I see it!" the wingman answered. He zoomed his P-38 upwards, chasing the Hamp for a thousand feet before the Japanese fighter veered sharply and zoomed downward— right into the 50-caliber sights of Colonel Bob Morrissey. The 49th Fighter Group commander pressed the buttons of his nose guns. The Hamp disintegrated like a shattered clay pigeon. The pieces dropped into the clouds.

Suddenly, the colonel's wingman found an angry Hamp on his tail. The Lightning pilot zigged and zagged, barrel rolled, dipped, and then zoomed upwards. But he could not shake off the persistent Hamp pilot. Intermittent 30-caliber bursts struck the twin fuselage: a chunk of tail, a slice of aileron, a piece of fuselage. Only the sturdiness of the American plane and the skill of the American pilot kept the Lightning aloft.

"Colonel! Colonel! Where the hell are you?" the wingman cried desperately.

But Colonel Morrissey was having difficulty in jockeying

into position for a shot at the Hamp. The Japanese interceptor banked and darted about the sky like an elusive sparrow, continuing to take pot shots at his quarry. Finally, a 30-caliber burst ignited a gas tank and Morrissey's wingman was finished. The flaming P-38 disappeared in a pall of fire and smoke into the clouds.

Morrissey cursed. He and his pilots had become dizzy and nauseous from the constant fight with enemy interceptors. Still the P-38 pilots fought on. And, despite their near exhaustion, they had scored 16 kills to a pair of losses of their own. Finally, the Hamp fighter unit, dismayed by their losses, scooted out of sight, away from any further fight.

Morrissey and his pilots of the 49th and 35th Fighter Groups had won respite for a few moments, enough time to catch their breath and clear the dizziness from their heads. But then Morrissey started when he peered to the northeast. "Good God! We must be over a breeding ground!"

A third wave of protecting Hamps were squealing into the dogfight area. But where had this third wave of Hamps been when the first two waves had engaged the P-38's earlier? The Japanese had apparently faulted again. They had come in one group at a time, allowing Morrissey and his pilots to enjoy a field day, before they were asked to take on another group.

"This is White Leader to all pilots! White Leader! Here they come again! Scramble by twos!"

The hovering P-38's circled before straightening in tight blocks of twos. Then the twenty-nine surviving P-38's zoomed northwestward into the enemy fighters. Like two bands of bloodthirsty hawks, the opposing aircraft clashed furiously. The concussing chatter of 50-caliber rounds mixed with the 30-caliber rounds of Japanese fighter planes echoed in the sky as the opposing units sprayed each other with tracer fire.

But the American pilots were more adept, their guns released stronger firepower, their planes absorbed harder punishment. The P-38's could climb faster and move at higher speeds. These advantages outweighed the better maneuverability of the Japanese Hamp fighter planes.

The fight high above the clouds over Huon Gulf had seen the Japanese pilots revert to form. Both General Ota Rampei, commander of the 7th Air Division in New Guinea, and Colonel Hato Shinohara, commander of the 7th Fighter Command, had promised that the sky over Huon Gulf would be like a skyful of locusts.

However, the Japanese had been unable to break their old habit of committing their aircraft in piecemeal fashion. More than a hundred Japanese fighter planes had loitered above the clouds to take on a mere 30-odd American fighter planes. Still, only a squadron at a time, 24 planes, came after the P-38's. This new batch of Hamps, just sighted to the northeast by Colonel Morrissey, would be no match for the Lightnings, which had already disposed of two earlier squadrons of Hamps. Worse, the enemy squadron could not count on help from the preceding squadrons already decimated by the Fifth Air Force fighter pilots.

This third fight, short and vicious, ended quickly. Within five minutes Colonel Morrissey and his pilots knocked 8 Hamps out of the sky and the surviving 16 Hamps veered sharply in a 180-degree arc and scurried northwestward. So the triumphant P-38 pilots, although dog tired, had finished off 24 Hamps and were now regrouping, catching a new snatch of rest, and waiting for the next wave of Hamps—one that would never come, because General Whitehead had checkmated the Japanese.

Bob Morrissey radioed Ed Larner. "We're still okay up here. We just chased off our third assault. We're tired as hell, but we'll be ready for the next wave."

"I don't think you'll see anymore," Larner said.

ED LARNER WAS FULLY AWARE of the reason. He knew that General Whitehead had instituted another tactic to heighten the chance of success for this second skip bomb strike against the Lae Resupply Convoy. The ADVON Fifth Air Force commander, in contrast to the hesitant Japanese, had cleaned house. Even though every available fighter plane had been sent on escort duty with the bombers, Whitehead did not leave his other bombers idle.

As soon as the skip bombers left Dobodura, he had sent out the twenty Boston and Beaufort light bombers of the Australian 9th Operational Group to hit Gasmata, directly across the Solomon Sea from Tufi. Whitehead had also sent a dozen B-25's from the 38th American Bomb Group scooting northward to Madang. Although Whitehead clearly recognized the danger of such raids without fighter escort, he chose to gamble. He hoped the bombers could make a quick strike against Gasmata and Madang and escape before they got jumped by Japanese interceptors.

The gamble had paid off. The two bomb groups had repeated with equal success the same technique they had used earlier in the day against Lae. The Beauforts and Bostons had skimmed across the Solomon Sea into Gasmata at sea level with parachute frag bombs and napalm gasoline bombs to hit the Gasmata airfields where three squadrons of Zeros were waiting to join the action over Huon Gulf. The Aussie pilots had caught dozens of fighter planes in the open and destroyed many of them in a quick strike. They had also potholed the Gasmata runways with their frag clusters so that even those planes that had escaped the napalm attack could never get into the air. Several hours would pass before Japanese service troops could patch up the airstrips to enable these planes from Gasmata to join the battle over Huon Gulf. By then the fight would surely be over.

The 38th Bomb Group's B-25's, carrying even heavier payloads, delivered a solid, unexpected blow at Madang. As with Gasmata, three squadrons of Japanese fighter planes were waiting for the word to join the fight in Huon Gulf. But the B-25's came in swiftly at low level, tree top, with parachute and napalm bombs. They left the airstrips dotted with potholes, unusable for several hours. They also destroyed many of the three squadrons of Japanese fighter planes that Admiral Kasaka had proudly proclaimed would join the "swarm of locusts" over Huon Gulf.

In both the Gasmata and Madang raids, the daring airmen, flying without fighter escort, had luckily met no Japanese interceptors. And, because of the sudden, devastating strikes, the spunky Allied pilots had deprived the Japanese of nearly 150 fighter planes to join the melee over Huon Gulf.

Ed Larner, then, could accurately tell Bob Morrissey that the fighter group commander might not meet any more Japanese interceptors. However, the major cautioned Morrissey not to pursue any fleeing Japanese fighter planes. The P-38's were to remain in their position above the clouds just in case. The major could be wrong and perhaps more enemy Hamps might show up and try to dive through the clouds to hit the bombers below.

Morrissey agreed and, in all truth, his pilots welcomed the rest from three Hamp assaults. They were content now to cruise lazily above the clouds to protect the bombers, if necessary.

Below the dense overcast, the P-40 pilots of the 9th RAAF and the 49th Fighter Group had enjoyed the same success against Japanese Zeros as Morrissey had enjoyed against the high-altitude Hamps. Here, too, the Japanese had clung to their habit of cautiousness. They had sent in their Zeros in piecemeal fashion, one squadron at a time, fighting the P-40 pilots on even terms. The equal fight had proved fatal.

Although the 49th Group had lost four P-40's to Zero fighters, the Warhawk pilots had downed 18 enemy planes, only six less than the P-38 pilots above the clouds. The Aussie P-40 unit had not lost any of the Warhawks.

Only eleven Japanese interceptor planes had managed to penetrate the guarding P-40's and P-38's to attack the bombers. But the infiltrating Hamps and Zeros had paid dearly for the privilege. Besides Cardis's kill, two other bomber pilots had shot down Zero interceptors. And the covering flight of Australian Beaufighters and 35th Fighter Group P38's around the bombers had accounted for six more Japanese fighter planes. Thus, only two of the eleven penetrating planes had survived.

But worse for the Japanese, the nine Zeros had caused minimal damage—only some 30-caliber puncture holes in the hulls of the A-20's and B-25's. None of the bombers would miss the attack on the convoy.

The Allied fighter planes, in downing or scattering the air cover of the Lae Resupply Convoy, had left the battered convoy wide open for the kill. Larner and his crews would not have to worry about interceptors while hitting their target.

Now, the P-38's above the clouds, the P-40's under the clouds, and the escort planes ringing the 3rd Bomb Group skip bombers would hover around the perimeter of the target area, on guard against interceptors, and later join strafing runs on the survivors of any sunken ships.

Still, Sergeant Joe Cardis felt a sense of uncertainty as the bomber formations moved closer to the Huon Gulf targets. He could not be sure that the danger of enemy interceptors was over—not after a half hour of deafening whines, thundering guns, flashing enemy planes, and arching American fighters. But he tried to relax during the final lap through the misty flight lane just above the choppy sea. He watched the P-40's join the Australian Beaufighters and American P-39's around the Mitchells before the combined force of escort planes leveled off and cruised alongside the 3rd Group bombers.

"This is Alpine Leader to all units; Alpine Leader to all units," Larner barked into his radio. "Get ready to scramble. Target in three minutes!"

Cardis pursed his lips, not so much with fear now but with anticipation. He squirmed in his bubble seat and then swung about in his turret until he was peering straight into the grayness ahead.

"Alpine leader to Gray Leader," Larner called the 35th Fighter Group commander. "What's ahead?"

Gray Leader, Major Martin, answered. "Area free and clear. Target scattered from eleven to one o'clock. You'll see them scooting around like crazy otters."

"Any interceptors?"

"Negative."

Larner checked with Colonel Bob Morrissey high above the clouds. There were no fighter planes upstairs either.

One can only wonder about the disappearance of Japanese fighter planes, and wonder about Colonel Hato Shinohara's pledge that no bomber would reach the Lae Resupply Convoy a second time. True, bombers from the 38th and 9th Groups had destroyed or grounded a large number of aircraft at Gasmata and Madang. But several squadrons of Hamps and Zeros had been airborne to engage the outnumbered Allied escorts. But apparently even the erstwhile Colonel Shinohara could not induce his squadron commanders to avoid the entrenched custom of piecemeal commitment. So the Japanese had lost some fifty aircraft in their poorly executed defense of the convoy.

In a postwar interview, Admiral Jinichi Kasaka was to concede two major faults of Japan's air arm: the failure to adequately train pilots and the unwillingness of commanders to attack en masse.

Colonel Shinohara also admitted that his pilots from Madang and Gasmata had been inept against the Allied fighter pilots. When losses became heavy, squadron flight leaders had simply withdrawn to avoid further losses.

So on the dark afternoon of 3 March 1943, after six blistering dogfights above and below the clouds, the protective air cover that Admiral Kimura needed so badly had all but disappeared. The "Eel of the Pacific" would once more have to fend for himself—and his prospects for escape were minimal.

Kimura's helmsmen and antiaircraft gunners would be forced to carry the burden once again. And, as Major Ed Larner's lead plane raced forward towards the scattered convoy, the plane suddenly shuddered from an ack-ack burst only a dozen yards away at two o'clock.

"There they are, Sal," Larner said, his voice low, almost hushed.

Lieutenant Dineo squinted out his cabin window and looked down at the sea. He stared hard at the twisting and turning patterns of the twelve surviving surface ships. The haphazard formation reminded him of confused acrobats who had missed their cues. It was almost laughable.

From his turret position, Joe Cardis felt a sudden compassion for the enemy vessels on the surface of Huon Gulf. To the young non-com, the frantically scattering ships were helpless sperm whales ripe for slaughter.

Chapter Fourteen

ROUND 3: THE DEATH BLOW

The twelve ships on Huon Gulf, some damaged, did not present the same rich target as the tied-up battleships at Pearl Harbor some fifteen months earlier. And in stark contrast to the surprised American military personnel on that 7 December 1941, those aboard the Lae Resupply Convoy knew the bombers were coming. The losses so far had almost equalled in numbers the total of ships lost at Pearl Harbor, and the sailors and soldiers of Kimura's convoy might have been wondering if they would be the victims of the highest surface ship losses in any single World War II engagement.

Even as some antiaircraft crews had begun to challenge the oncoming bombers, other antiaircraft gunners had assembled in quick conferences aboard the Japanese vessels to plan strategy against the water-skimming bombers. They called on technicians who worked feverishly to adjust gun fulcrums so the gunners could shoot point-blank into the surface of the sea and hit the skimming bombers coming in just above the whitecapped crests of Huon Gulf.

From the wheelhouse of the *Shirayuki*, Admiral Kimura

stared at the drab gray clouds above the sea. Gone were the swarms of protective Zero and Hamp fighter planes except for an occasional sortie that dipped out of the low mist for a gun-rattling moment before disappearing back into the clouds. Gone was the hope of new protection from Madang or Gasmata. Radio reports had told Kimura that American B-25's and Australian Beauforts had struck both bases with devastating results.

The admiral stood erect, his face hard, his dark eyes reflecting a trace of defiance, the pride of a man who had given his utmost. Doubt radiated through his mind. The American skip bombers zooming towards Huon Gulf would decimate them just as they had before. The Eleventh Air Fleet in Rabaul and Kavieng were hours away from the fight, and they might only find a choppy sea and boiling clouds—if and when they got here.

Suddenly a messenger burst into the wheelhouse. "Admiral, enemy aircraft reported off port, bearing one-nine-zero."

Kimura simply nodded and walked to the foredeck of the bridge. Captain Tishayuna trailed after him while the helmsman followed both officers with his eyes. No one said anything.

Kimura raised his field glasses and peered into the eastern horizon. The B-25's were charging like angry hawks. Kimura frowned as the convoy's ack-ack guns came alive. The rattled gunners, panicky, were defeating themselves. Flak exploded around the bombers with pitiful inaccuracy—too high, too wide, too short. The American aircraft never budged from their tight diamond formations.

"Alpine Leader to all units!" Major Larner cried into his radio. "Convoy ahead! Ready for scramble in sixty seconds . . . sixty seconds. And remember, in pairs and fifteen seconds apart. Choose your targets and hit in pairs!"

Larner fixed his eyes on the *Shirayuki*, Admiral Kimura's flagship. "Wing," he called into his radio, "we're going after that cruiser! Follow me in at five hundred yards!"

A moment later, Larner leaned forward in his pilot's seat. Again he spoke into his radio: "All units, all units! On the ready—*scramble!*"

The neat pattern of diamonds broke. In pairs, the Mitchells skimmed towards the scattered Lae Resupply

Convoy. From 2nd Flight, Captain Don McNutt and his wingman veered at eleven o'clock, while the major and his wingman veered to one o'clock. Larner dropped *Spook* to almost 25 feet and roared towards the cruiser, his eyes narrowed in determination, his mouth dry with nervous anticipation. He curled his hand in readiness over the bomb release button.

Dineo, next to Larner, stared intently at the flopping *Shirayuki.* The big cruiser was listing from port to starboard and back, repeatedly, in desperate, zig-zagging turns. Its bow kicked up salt water geysers, its stern exploded foaming sprays, even as its pom-pom gunners, poured frantic fire into the approaching Mitchells. But, as before, the 20MM rounds whooshed too far above the onrushing B-25.

ABOARD THE *SHIRAYUKI,* ADMIRAL KIMURA stood defiantly on the bridge. "To port! 90 degrees to port!" he yelled. And as the sleek cruiser veered, Larner arched his plane and banked the B-25 squarely at the port side. When *Spook* came to within 50 yards of the *Shirayuki,* Kimura took a tight grip on the bridge railing, bracing himself for the hit.

Larner slammed the release button with the palm of his hand. Two skip bombs dropped out of the Mitchell's bomb bay and skimmed towards the forward port of the cruiser. Admiral Kimura heard the straining whine as Larner's B-25 arched upward and away from the cruiser. The Japanese commander caught but a glimpse of the white letters on the side of the rising aircraft—S-P-O-O-K—a split second before the skip bombs slammed into his ship and tore his grip from the railing. The twin concussions flung the admiral across the bridge deck in a skidding circle and he fell on his side, stunned but not hurt.

Kimura struggled to his feet as the *Shirayuki* began listing to port. He squinted to his right, but saw only the wall of smoke pouring from the side of the convoy's flagship. "Damage! Damage control! Get damage control!"

But suddenly, two more deafening explosions bounced him off his feet, and he again skidded across the tilted bridge deck. Then the blare of whoop alarms numbed Kimura's ear drums. He tried to scramble once more to his feet, but the *Shirayuki* was nearly at a 20-degree slant and still listing. Suddenly, the Japanese fleet commander heard the shrill voice of a security officer calling urgently.

"Abandon ship! Abandon ship!"

Kimura's dark eyes raced about the deck until they fell on Captain Tishayuna. The executive officer was lying against the starboard bulkhead of the wheelhouse, struggling to get to his feet. The admiral quickly crawled over to him. "Captain! Captain Tishayuna!"

Tishayuna rolled over weakly and looked up at his commander. His face was ashen, his eyes dull. "All is lost, Admiral Kimura, all is lost."

The executive officer's moans of resigned defeat erupted a fury in Admiral Kimura. Captain Tishayuna suddenly saw a stranger looming over him, a man who resembled some angry samurai ancestor. Blazing anger beamed out of the admiral's normally quiet eyes. Kimura's calm face had hardened into one of those distorted paste masks so often seen in the Tokyo festival parades. And even the veins of the admiral's hands were cutting through the skin, a hint that infuriation mixed with frustration had gripped the commander of the Lae Resupply Convoy.

Captain Tishayuna had never seen such emotion in the man he had followed faithfully since they left Tokyo nearly a year ago to join the Eighth Fleet. But then, in a year of combat, Admiral Kimura had never before found himself teetering on the brink of total defeat. As an executive officer aboard one of the ships in the Battle of Midway, Kimura had only seen localized glimpses of the action and the impact of the Midway battle had held little meaning for him. And next, as commander of convoy armadas to the Philippines, to Southeast Asia, or to the East Indies, he had never met serious resistance. He had easily disposed of or chased off the obsolete American submarines or the weak elements of the British and Dutch navies that had tried to stop him. He had handily avoided the futile Allied attempts to hit him with a handful of worn-out planes.

And, of course, Kimura had been the hero of the Solomon Islands campaign, despite the Japanese loss of Guadalcanal and Bougainville. Not only Captain Tishayuna, but other Japanese naval officers knew that no naval commander had enjoyed the success of Kimura in maneuvering through Ironbottom Strait. He had foxily eluded Allied sea and air units to unload Japanese troop reinforcements and had then returned unscathed to the safety of Rabaul.

Kimura's daring and cunning for more than a year had certainly entitled him to the respected title—Eel of the Pacific. Every staff member at Japanese Imperial Headquarters in Rabaul believed that Kimura could lead safely this Lae Resupply Convoy to New Guinea as he had earlier guided a smaller convoy safely to New Guinea in January, despite growing Allied air strength in Papua. The success of the January mission had been the final triumph that had made Kimura an idol in the eyes of every warrior of Nippon in the Southwest Pacific area. With the planning of Operation 157, all hands, from the lowest Japanese soldier to the highest Japanese admiral, had welcomed the appointment of Kimura as the commander of the critical Lae Resupply Convoy.

Perhaps Kimura himself had come to believe in his own invincibility. And so, on this late afternoon of 3 March 1943, with the spectre of inevitable disaster, Kimura's composure had disintegrated. Perhaps he could not yet believe as he hung desperately to the gunwale railing that his proud cruiser was listing more and more to port, belching and hissing before it took its final plunge to the bottom of Huon Gulf. Perhaps Kimura was shocked to hear his executive officer, who had always praised his successes, now lament the failure with words alien to samurai tradition: "All is lost."

Kimura looked down at his executive officer and glared before he spoke in a tone that was utterly out of character.

"Who gave the order to abandon ship? Who?" he growled.

But Tishayuna, despite his uneasiness with Kimura's anger, answered in the same discouraging wail. "It will be of no consequences, Honorable Admiral. All is lost."

Anger again reddened Kimura's face. "Are you a lamb that you speak so?" Then, in a move that was also out of Kimura's character, the admiral yanked Tishayuna to his feet and half slammed him against a bulkhead. "Not until we have expended our last breath is all lost. If you are not injured, see quickly what can be done."

The admiral's sharp retort shook Tishayuna from his submissive despair. The executive officer saw that Kimura, despite the agony confronting him, had mustered courage during obvious defeat just as he had so often displayed modesty during his many military successes. Tishayuna stiffened and faced his admiral stoically.

"Forgive me, Kimura-*san.* I spoke recklessly. I will do what I can in this crisis."

Kimura nodded, released his executive officer, and then catpawed along the inclined deck towards the wheelhouse. He slid along the slanted steel wall to remain erect until he lurched through the open door of the cabin. The helmsman, striving to stay on his feet, held firmly to the wheel, straining to veer the big cruiser to starboard and thus slow down the rapid port list. Occasionally, the helmsman cringed from the spirals of smoke curling up from the port beam.

"A true samurai," Kimura tapped the helmsman on the shoulder.

The admiral clung to a bulkhead grip and squinted through the palls of smoke beyond the wheelhouse. Then he jerked as the whoop alarm again echoed through the ship. Tishayuna was right; they could not save the proud cruiser. Kimura picked up a JV phone and called the security area.

"What is our condition?"

But the admiral heard only the worst from a security officer. The entire port side of the *Shirayuki* had been ripped open by skip bombs. Tons of water were pouring into the port side hull with no chance to stop it. Repair crews had opened starboard compartments in an attempt to right the vessels for easier abandonment of ship. The ship was lost as were dozens of Japanese sailors and the chief security officer himself, Captain Yusi Watanabe.

"I implore you, Admiral," the security officer pleaded over the JV phone, "Leave the bridge at once. We can estimate no more than ten minutes before the vessel sinks. Even now the *Shikanami* comes towards us to retrieve survivors."

Kimura sighed, laid down the JV phone, then looked wistfully at the pall of smoke beyond the wheelhouse. The admiral, now accepting the obvious, and doing his best in defeat as he had so often done in victory, had reverted to his calm, composed self. He ordered the security officer to lower the longboats and to remove from the sinking ship every sailor on board. He then turned to the helmsman who still clung tenaciously to his post.

"Tie the wheel to a bulkhead and then hurry to a longboat."

"I will stay with my admiral."

"You will tie the wheel and leave."

The helmsman hesitated, then quickly took a line. With the aid of Kimura, the helmsman tied the line from the full-turned wheel to a bulkhead, locking the ship on a wide, counterclockwise, circular course. The technique did slow the portside list and thus afforded an easier abandonment of the ship.

When Kimura cocked his head, the helmsman bowed before the admiral and scrambled out of the tilted cabin. A moment later, after he had taken one final check of the wheelhouse, Kimura, too, left the cabin. He weaved atilt along the bridge deck, staggering as though intoxicated, until he saw Captain Tishayuna. The executive officer had also regained his composure and was calmly directing sailors into a lifeboat. When he saw the admiral, the captain gestured to a subordinate to continue operations. Then he turned to his commander.

"The *Shikanami* will soon be alongside to retrieve survivors. We shall make every attempt to save all who still breathe. I urge you, Admiral, please join the others in the longboats and transfer your flag to the *Shikanami*."

Before Kimura could respond, a B-25 whined towards the stricken *Shirayuki*. Both officers looked skyward and then quickly dropped in huddled crouches as the Mitchell dove towards the cruiser. The pilot released no skip bombs, but he did press the button of his nose cannons. Tracers ripped into the starboard side of the cruiser, chopping away chunks of metal, riddling two of the lifeboats, shooting up pom-pom emplacements, and killing and wounding numerous sailors.

When the deadly chatter of the nose guns stopped, Kimura leaped to his feet to see the bomber whisk across the *Shirayuki's* superstructure. As the B-25 banked away from the ship and zoomed off, he knew instinctively that the pilot would be wasting no more bombs on the *Shirayuki*. One pass over the listing warship had obviously convinced the pilot of the cruiser's doom.

AS FRIGHTENED, DAZED, AND INJURED SAILORS abandoned the convoy's flag cruiser, and Ed Larner sought more targets, companion B-25's of the 90th Squadron were attacking other vessels. Captain Don McNutt of the squadron's 2nd Flight roared into the stern of the zig-zagging destroyer *Tokitsukaze*. The slim ship churned exploding wakes as it plowed full speed through the choppy Gulf. The stern gunners fired frantically at the approaching B-25, but McNutt was skimming well under the murderous barrages.

Within 400 yards, McNutt pressed the triggers of his nose guns. Streams of 50-caliber rounds poured into the *Tokitsukaze's* poop gun pits. One burst struck a stack of 20MM ammo, and the gun pit and its crew disappeared in a spectacular explosion. As tracers ripped into the other gun pits, the gunners panicked and scurried away from their stations.

McNutt tried to maneuver his Mitchell into skip bomb position, but the destroyer was too elusive. The B-25 overshot the ship and the skip bombs sailed over the stern and exploded in the sea. However, McNutt's wingman had slipped neatly up to the starboard side of the destroyer. The ship tried desperately to wheel to port, but the 90th Squadron pilot unleashed two skip bombs within 25 yards of the vessel's exposed beam. As the five-hundred pounders streaked into the waterline of the ship, the B-25 bellied up over the destroyer and strained skyward.

The double explosion sent metal debris scattering in a lethal, shotgun pattern. While the ship was still shuddering, McNutt banked in a wide turn and slammed his second pair of skip bombs into the *Tokitsukaze's* stern. The bombs struck the destroyer starboard aft.

As gushing sea water poured into the aft, the bow of the destroyer jerked out of the water like the prow of a surfacing submarine. When McNutt's wingman sent two more skip bombs into the destroyer's port aft, the destroyer plunged under the murky waters of Huon Gulf, stern first. Within minutes, only debris and bobbing heads lay on the surface of the sea, including that of General Hatazo Adachi. Fortunately, the Eighteenth Army commander and most of his staff were rescued by the destroyer *Shikanami*.

A transport was the next victim. It was a *maru* crowded with its own troop complement and some rescued 51st Division personnel. 3rd Flight of the 90th Squadron ganged up on the helpless vessel like preying hawks pouncing on a crazed rabbit. The transport veered and plowed frantically, its ack-ack gunners firing furiously. But again, the popping five-inch flak burst too far above the low-level aircraft. In desperation, the Japanese even fired rifles and 30-caliber machine guns at the B-25's. But a sudden burst of nose fifties from the Mitchells scattered the brazen effort.

One of the Mitchells dived at the starboard side, raking the decks with 50-caliber rounds before unleashing its skip bombs. The next two B-25's of the abbreviated three-plane 3rd Flight sailed four skip bombs into the starboard waterline. In seconds, the entire side of the transport was a pall of smoke. The B-25's arched in a 180-degree turn, skimmed back at the vessel's port side and loosened their second skip bomb attack on the port beam. Three of the second six bombs hit the target, causing more explosions. Soon a thick wad of smoke enveloped the transport until the airmen above saw only a black, oblong cloud on the surface of the sea. As the smoke dimmed, the transport settled slowly to the bottom of Huon Gulf.

Finally the last two B-25's of the 90th Squadron's eleven planes arched towards the destroyer *Uranami*. The warship had lost its forward gun mounts to the 38th Bomb Group the day before. As two B-25's came in on the forward starboard, a barrage of pom-pom and five-inch antiaircraft shells from beam and aft guns exploded erratically in harmless black puff above the skimming B-25's.

At 400 yards, the B-25 pilots loosed a stream of nose gun tracers to disrupt the wheelhouse crew. However, the *Uranami* helmsman, reacting quickly to orders, had made a quick ninety-degree turn as the Mitchells unleashed their skip bombs within 50 yards of the starboard hull. The skip bombs fell short and exploded huge balls of foaming sea. The *Uranami* would live to fight again.

However, the convoy lost another of its freighters as a flight of A-20's from the 89th Squadron raked a damaged cargo vessel with strafing fire. Before the A-20's had even released their skip bombs, some of the tracer rounds had struck the vessel's magazine, turning the poop deck into a huge ball of orange fire. The stern settled quickly under the sea.

The three A-20's veered away for a moment but quickly returned and leaped on the wounded cargo ship like hungry pelicans after an injured fish. They struck both port and starboard bows, chopping out huge gaps in the hull. The ship disappeared altogether under Huon Gulf following a final explosion.

The last freighter also fell victim to the A-20 Havocs of the 89th Squadron. But, as a consolation, the gunners of a destroyer had knocked two of the A-20's out of the air before surrendering their freighter-ward to the skip bombers.

Finally, the huge *Teiyo Maru*, crowded with 6,000 men, including those rescued from other ships, fell victim to the A-20's. The Havocs opened up her entire port side with skip bombs and the big transport went down with 1,600 men. This final blow had been the worst of all in the loss of men. Fortunately, the adept destroyer crews rescued hundreds of men from the sea.

Major Ed Larner, still hoping to hit the remaining targets, now called on his own flight leaders and Major Glen Clark of the 89th Squadron. But the major soon learned that the eleven B-25's and the fifteen A-20's of the 3rd Bomb Group skip bombers had expended their bombs while sending a destroyer, a cruiser, two freighters and two transports to the bottom of Huon Gulf. Now, only one dazed transport and five destroyers still slopped about Huon Gulf. Still, Larner growled in disappointment. These last six ships, especially the transport, would have been easy targets.

HOWEVER, LARNER AND HIS FLIGHT CREWS, as well as the escorting fighter pilots, had to do something about the hundreds of heads bobbing on the surface of Huon Gulf.

The 90th Squadron commander did not appreciate the savage task. But, he knew the potential consequences against Allied infantrymen. Grimly, the major picked up his radio.

"This is Alpine Leader. All units, report."

"One transport," a flight leader answered.

"We got a freighter," another pilot said.

"A tin can," Captain McNutt said.

"Any signs of interceptors?" Larner now called into his radio.

"Nothing."

No, there were no interceptors near the dismembered convoy. There were no Zeros under the clouds. Only P-40's, and P-39's, and Beaufighters flitted between the low-hanging clouds and the surface of the sea. And when Major Ed Larner called Colonel Bob Morrissey, the White Leader also answered in the negative: no Hamps above the clouds. In fact, there had not been any Hamps about for ten minutes, according to the 49th Fighter Group commander.

"Okay," Larner told Morrissey. "Leave some P-38's upstairs on alert and the rest of you can come down for strafing runs." Larner also gave permission to the fighter planes under the clouds to join the same task.

In moments, the P-40's, P-39's, and Beaufighters dove towards the decimated convoy. Minutes later, Colonel Bob Morrissey's P-38's dipped out of the clouds and joined the action on the surface of Huon Gulf. The rattle of machine guns echoed across the choppy waters as the Warhawks, Lightnings, Beaufighters and Aeracobras joined the B-25's and A-20's in the murderous strafing runs.

After the array of Allied fighters and bombers had sprayed the sea for more than ten minutes, Larner called into his radio. "This is Alpine Leader to all units! Gray and White Leaders, cease fire! Cease Fire! You too, Diggers."

"There's a lot of work still to be done, Matey," one of the RAAF squadron leaders told Larner, "and we've still got plenty of rounds."

But Larner would have no more. The bombers might need the guns of the fighter escorts in case any Hamps or Zeros jumped them on the way home. He again called into his radio. "Gray and White Leaders, please rendezvous for return to base. I'll be along. Out."

As the Allied aircraft moved into formation, Major Larner circled around the sea to study results. The 90th Squadron commander caught a glimpse of the *Shirayuki's* pagoda mast before the big ship disappeared under Huon Gulf. Then, he saw the listing transport and the destroyers *Shikanami* and *Asagumo* plucking survivors from the sea. (Admiral Kimura was rescued.) Larner dipped closer to the rescuing destroyers to get a closer look at the Japanese salvage operations. However, in a final determined effort, the destroyers' gunners unleashed a heavy barrage of ack-ack fire and Larner was forced to zoom away and out of danger.

In other parts of Huon Gulf, other destroyers were also pulling survivors from the sea.

Admiral Kimura watched the Allied planes disappear into the horizon, then climbed a rope ladder to board the *Shikanami.* The admiral felt a mixture of relief and anger. The marauders were gone but so was most of the Lae

Resupply Convoy. The day indeed belonged to the Allies.

Long after Larner and his air crews had left Huon Gulf, the Japanese destroyers continued to rescue sailors and soldiers from the sea: those who had first escaped their sinking ships and then the murderous Allied strafing. The rescuers found men clinging to debris, huddled in overcrowded lifeboats, or desperately treading water. It would be dusk before the destroyers and damaged transport left the Huon Gulf disaster area.

Hundreds of experienced Japanese sailors had died. Badly needed supplies and oil would not reach New Guinea, and thousands of reinforcements would not reach New Guinea. The ships, merchantmen as well as warships, could never be replaced. By 1900 hours, friend and foe alike knew of the great disaster that had struck the armada that was supposed to have provided the material and men needed to insure victory in New Guinea and, thus, render Australia vulnerable to invasion.

Chapter Fifteen

TO THE VICTORS. . . .

The bomber and fighter strips at Dobodura were not the elaborate runways of the Le Bourget Airport in Paris on that day in May, 1927, when Lindbergh completed his solo flight across the Atlantic. And the size of the crowd in the jungle certainly did not match those who greeted Lindbergh. But MP's and air service guards struggled to stem the crowds pressing around the airstrip. The waiting crowds occupied every square foot of space along the runways and taxi ways. They milled about in massive groups; they sat in jammed bunches atop six-by-sixes, jeeps, and other available vehicles; many sat in rows atop the dirt revetment dunes of aircraft shelters; still others sat atop the wings of idle aircraft.

At 1815 hours, the first dots emerged from the darkening sky above the Solomon Sea. The control tower operator at Dobodura immediately contacted Major Ed Larner for a report on damage and casualties. They did not require crash trucks, Larner said, for they expected no planes to come in with damaged landing gears, shot-up tails, lacerated wings, or knocked-out engines. Larner, however, did report several wounded aboard some of the returning 3rd Group aircraft and these crewmen would need medical help. So far as Larner knew, none of the returning fighter pilots were injured.

"What about the Aussies?"

"They're okay," Larner answered the control towers. "Their three fighter squadrons are going to Wau."

As Larner settled the first returning B-25 on the dirt runway and rolled to the far end of the strip, air service guards and MP's could not restrain the crowd. Three vehicles wheeled onto the airstrip and roared after *Spook*, ignoring the clouds of dust from the B-25's slip stream. Behind the vehicles swarms of men ran wildly down the runway. When *Spook* came to a stop, a dozen hands snapped open the belly hatches and ground crews literally dragged Larner and his two crewmen from the plane.

Dineo grinned as squadron comrades tossed him on their shoulders and carried him to a waiting jeep. Other ground crews personally hauled an astonished Joe Cardis to a command car, nearly ripping off his flying gear in the process.

Pappy Gunn, who had flown in from Port Moresby as soon as the 3rd Group took off, forced his way through the mob and vigorously pumped the hand of Ed Larner. "We did it, boy! We did it!"

"The general ought to be happy now," Larner grinned.

Gunn gave a chomp on his cigar and grinned. "He wants to see us. I think he's got a drawer full of medals for us."

Then, Larner, like his crew, was swept up in a swarm of well wishers.

Nor were the crews of other returning B-25's and A-20's ignored. And the fighter pilots who had knocked most of the defending Japanese cover out of the air were also deluged by enthusiastic crowds. Men and vehicles chased after these planes and ripped open the hatches of the bombers or pulled open the cockpit canopies of fighter planes to drag, carry, or haul the bomber crews and fighter pilots to waiting vehicles.

In this jungle air base, where flights to and from a mission bordered on the routine, the bedlam was unique. But every airman and soldier in Dobodura knew the significance of these returning planes: The Japanese would not mount a ground offensive; their base on New Guinea had been saved—perhaps even their lives!

At Wau, practically every soldier of the Kanga Force crowded the small dirt runway to hail their own fighter pilots of the 75th, 77th, and 30th Fighter Squadrons. No group of men could feel more grateful than these Diggers at Wau over the destruction of the Lae Resupply Convoy. The soldiers of the Kanga Force knew the meaning of the debacle on Huon Gulf better than anyone else: For a long, long time, no Japanese attackers would pour out of the gloomy forests to strike at their defense perimeter.

The Aussie pilots came into the Wau airstrip carefully, like aircraft carrier pilots. They hit the runway squarely, for crowds of men had lined both sides of the strip. When a fighter pilot fantailed his plane to a stop, Aussie Diggers swarmed over the plane and, like the Americans at Dobodura, ripped back the canopy of the fighter plane and dragged the pilot from the cockpit.

Yet, the elated Aussie fighter pilots modestly credited their bomb crews of the 9th Operational Group who had struck hard at Gasmata to prevent further Japanese interceptors from joining the melee over Huon Gulf.

"We were dead tired, we were," one pilot summarized. "If our blokes didn't bloody well maul 'em at Ga'mata, we might have been done in. And we can thank those Yanks who hit Madang, too."

At Port Moresby, the tensions and uncertainties had ended. The old hotel offices of Fifth Air Force ADVON Headquarters had become bedlam with wild, screaming celebrations, and a new cheer every time somebody posted another tally on the chalkboard. Outside, in the growing dusk, personnel had again massed themselves before the dilapidated porch. They milled about eagerly until a sergeant in an excited voice told them it was all over: the convoy was destroyed. For one brief moment, a stunned silence gripped the mob, but then an explosion of cheers rattled the old hotel. The men at Moresby, Australians and Americans alike, jostled each other in feverish celebration. Tonight they would release three days of tension with jungle juice parties in every tented campsite.

General Whitehead himself had been speaking to General George Kenney at Fifth Air Force Headquarters in Brisbane. Kenney had listened with the same awe and exhilaration, as did the lowest private in New Guinea. The

Japanese defeat in Operation Bismarck Sea had brought one certainty: the delicate stalemate in the Southwest Pacific had been shattered. From this moment on, the Japanese would be the defenders and the Allies would be the aggressors. But even more significant, air power had proven its worth. Operation Bismarck Sea would silence the critics who persistently claimed the air corps could only be a supporting arm for other branches of the military.

When General George Kenney released Whitehead's report on Operation Bismarck Sea, the streets of Brisbane, Australia, burst into wild celebration, a celebration that spread quickly throughout the rest of the Southern Cross continent. The threat of a Japanese invasion of Australia had ended with the final machine gun round over the surface of Huon Gulf.

In contrast, only glum despair radiated through the Japanese bases of the Bismarck Archipelago. Neither admirals, generals, nor the ranks of Japanese soldiers and sailors could fathom the stinging defeat: sixteen ships of an Imperial convoy sent to the bottom in a devastating two-day fight.

The destroyers *Uranami* and *Yukikaze* were plying back to Rabaul with some 1400 survivors, while the destroyer *Asagumo* was limping towards Kavieng with other survivors. Only the wounded transport *Oigawa Maru* and two destroyers, *Shikanami* and *Arishio* puffed into Lae. Dusk had settled over Lae Harbor and the dense clouds had again dissipated. The sun was sinking below the northernmost Mambare Mountain Range, leaving a dull orange hue in the darkening sky. Among the Japanese garrisons around the harbor, the atmosphere was as black as the night.

The three ships of Kimura's convoy that came to Lae anchored in the harbor, their personnel too spent and too shocked to disembark. They had given their all, fought with honor and courage, but it had not been enough. In the final hours, the gods—and the Japanese air force—had forsaken them. When the shore-based soldiers were certain that no one would come ashore that night, they ambled off in silent clusters to accept the bitter defeat as best they could.

The U. S. Navy dealt a final blow to the Lae Resupply Convoy. At 2200 hours on the evening of March 3, before the moon was up, four PT boats from the Seventh Fleet stole into

Lae Harbor. They unleashed a string of torpedoes that struck the *Oigawa Maru* broadside. The transport and some of her jammed human cargo sunk to the bottom of the harbor, but most of her passengers, 850 of them, managed to reach shore. These soldiers, along with General Hatazo Adachi and most of his staff, were all that reached their New Guinea destination.

The next morning, before the sun rose out of the Solomon Sea, a single B-17 soared over Lae Harbor and dropped four 1,000 pound bombs on one of the anchored destroyers, the *Arishio*. One bomb sailed into the ship's smokestack. The rattling explosion tore the vessel apart and the battered hulk was later beached. From the surviving destroyer *Shikanami*, Admiral Kimura, Captain Tishayuna, and General Adachi could only wonder if this morning blow had finally ended the nightmare.

Thus, of the 22-ship convoy that had left Rabaul on 28 February 1943, only the *Shikanami* anchored safely in Lae. And, ironically, the *Shikanami* would be the only warship of the four destroyers that survived the Bismarck Sea fight to also survive the war.

The *Uranami* would fight for another year before she was lost in the Battle of San Bernardino Strait. The *Asagumo* would sink in the Battle of Surigao Strait, and the *Hatsuyuki* would be beached after a bitter fight against American destroyers in the Sea of Japan in July, 1945, just before the war ended.

THE SUCCESS OF OPERATION BISMARCK SEA prompted General Douglas MacArthur to make this statement: "It was the most decisive aerial engagement in this theater of war."

General George E. Kenney also issued a statement: "Air power has proven its worth during these past three days. The air corps need no longer be considered a bridesmaid for other military departments."

Kenney had the right to make this boast, for the Bismarck Sea operation, utilizing air power alone, had sent more ships to the bottom than in any other single engagement of World War II. And, however late, Operation Bismarck Sea had finally vindicated General Billy Mitchell and other controversial air corps pioneers.

All participating Allied air groups in the battle received

presidential unit citations, and dozens of individual airmen received medals. They ranged from Distinguished Flying Crosses to Silver Stars to Bronze Stars to the Air Medal. Colonel Paul "Pappy" Gunn won both a Commendation Medal and the Legion of Merit for his skip bombing (as well as other gadgetry) innovation that proved so crucial to the battle. Major Ed Larner received both the DFC and Silver Star.

While the 26 bombers of the 3rd Bomb Group won high praise, Ed Larner was quick to point out that their victory was based on support received from other units. He compared his crews to football running backs who only succeed because of good linemen: the reconnaissance pilots who worked around the clock to keep the convoy in sight; the fighter pilots who kept away the swarms of Japanese interceptors; the other bomb groups who had struck Lae, Madang, and Gasmata; the bombers who had hit the convoy earlier; and the tremendous efforts and expertise of ground crews. He summed up that the Bismarck Sea triumph had been a coordinated Fifth Air Force effort and, perhaps luckily, had been directed by General Ennis Whitehead.

The aircraft involved in the fight had dropped 571 total bombs and had fired over 50,000 machine gun rounds. Of the fifty-seven 500-pound skip bombs dropped by 3rd Bomb Group, thirty-eight had struck home, accounting for thirteen sinkings. The Allied bombers and escorting fighters had encountered 350 Japanese interceptor planes during the three-day melee. Of these, Allied bomber crews and fighter plane pilots had claimed 100 to 120 kills, including those destroyed on the ground in Lae, Madang, and Gasmata. On the Allied side, they had lost eight aircraft: three bombers and five fighter planes. In total, the Allied aircraft had conducted over 400 sorties in the three-day engagement.

On the Japanese side, Imperial Eighth Area Headquarters denied the Allied claims that all but 900 of the 15,000 troops had been lost. They said destroyers had rescued over 5,000 men and submarines had plucked another 300 out of the sea.

NONETHELESS, THE LAE RESUPPLY CONVOY operation had been a disaster that ended any further Japanese offenses in New Guinea. Never again did the Japanese attempt to send troop transports or merchant ships into her New

Guinea bases from Rabaul. The Fifth Air Force had proven itself too potent. All further reinforcements in men and supplies came in by submarines or in barges at night down from Wewak and Madang. However, these improvised methods afforded only a trickle of help for General Adachi and he subsequently fought a losing, defensive war in New Guinea. Only a few months after Operation Bismarck Sea, the Allies took the offensive in the Southwest Pacific. Lae fell to General Douglas MacArthur's paratroopers in September, 1943, in the first thrust back to the Philippines.

As a result of the Lae Resupply Convoy debacle, both General Hitoshi Imamura and Admiral Jinichi Kasaka lost their commands. Tokyo blamed Imamura for poor planning and they blamed Kasaka for the air force ineffectiveness. General Adachi retained his Eighteenth Army command but he could not stem the turning tide. His New Guinea army was soon neutralized as an effective fighting force, and the proud Japanese commander eventually evacuated New Guinea. Admiral Gunichi Mikawa shifted his naval efforts elsewhere until finally, in late 1944, he suffered irreversible defeat in the naval battles around the Philippines that all but destroyed the Japanese navy.

Only Masatomi Kimura continued to distinguish himself. Japanese military leaders exonerated the "Eel of the Pacific." They decided that poor air support, lack of enough naval support, and the ineptness of General Imamura had caused the disaster to the Lae Resupply Convoy. Imperial Headquarters gave Admiral Kimura a new command, a cruiser attack force. At once, he reverted to his old cagey tactics. In retreat during 1943 and 1944, Kimura salvaged more soldier evacuees from New Guinea, the East Indies, and the Philippines than any other naval commander.

And while the rest of the Japanese navy was suffering annihilation in the ill-fated Sho Operation during the Battle for the Philippines, Admiral Kimura was still punching Allied forces. On Christmas day, 1944, the wily Kimura successfully entered San Jose Bay at Mindoro in the Philippines, with two cruisers and six destroyers. He gave the American invasion force an evening of heat, worry, and substantial losses in men and supplies. Then Kimura successfully eluded half the Fifth Air Force and a fleet of American submarines and surface warships to bring his small attack force safely back to Cam Ranh Bay in Indo-China. His attack force had been the only one to escape destruction in the Battle of the Philippines. So, Admiral Masatomi Kimura was still the slippery "Eel of the Pacific."

But Kimura's Mindoro foray was his last triumph. In early 1945, he returned to Japan to sit out the rest of the war at a desk job, a distasteful finish for the old seahorse. In his three years of war, nothing had impressed Kimura as much as the skip bomber. He wrote in his diary during the waning days of the war: "The Mitchell (B-25) is most terrifying. We could not adequately chase them off and we thus repeated the failure of Guadalcanal. Most regrettable."

Thus, the wily Admiral Masatomi Kimura had called the low-level attack bomber the most destructive weapon of the Pacific war.

General Ennis Whitehead, meanwhile, continued to direct the combat air groups of the Fifth Air Force: the Admiralties, the Philippines, Okinawa, and finally Japan itself. He reached the rank of Lieutenant General and commanded the Far East Air Forces by the end of the war. In 1945 he returned to the United States in triumph, his chest weighted down with medals as evidence of his worth as a tactical air force commander. He spent a few years at a desk job in the mishmash of the Pentagon, but it was not for him. In 1950, the old war hawk retired and fell into obscurity.

Both Pappy Gunn and Major Ed Larner returned to the United States by the end of 1943. Larner became an instructor for the hundreds of training airmen who would move into the Pacific to continue the war against Japan. Pappy Gunn put his ingenuity to work at Wright Field, introducing new innovations for combat aircraft. However, it was not the same for the two men who had met the hard challenge during those desperate early days in New Guinea. When the war ended, both men left the service.

New Guinea and New Britain are quiet now. The jungle has reclaimed the old Allied and Japanese air bases. The kunai grass has swallowed up the last evidences of the old airstrips at Dobodura, Wau, Tufi, Madang, Kavieng, Wewak, Cape Gloucester, and Gasmata. Only at Port Moresby, Lae, and Rabaul are airstrips still in service, but they only service small civilian aircraft.

The waters of the Bismarck Archipelago no longer echo

with the roar of naval guns, whistling bombs, and machine gun chatter. Only placid cargo ships and adventurous sloops carrying hemp, copra, rubber, and tourists ply the sea lanes of the Bismarck and Solomon Seas. Only the weather has not changed. A bright sunny day on the Bismarck Sea may, in minutes, change to a dull dark day of thunderstorms.

BIBLIOGRAPHY

BOOKS

Arnold, H. H. *War Reports*. Philadelphia: J. P. Lippincott, 1947.

Blair, Clay Jr. *Silent Victory*. New York: J. P. Lippincott, 1975.

Craven, William F. and Cate, J.L. *The Army Air Forces in World War II*. Vol. IV. The Pacific—Guadalcanal to Saipan, August 1942 to July 1944. Chicago: University of Chicago Press, 1964.

Janaka, Hato. *Japan's Losing Struggle for Guadalcanal*. Boston: Little Brown and Co., 1952.

Joblonski, Edward. *Flying Fortress*. Garden City: Doubleday and Co., 1965.

———. *Air War*. Garden City: Doubleday and Co., 1971.

Karig, Walter. *The End of an Empire*. Chicago: Chicago University Press, 1952.

MacArthur, Douglas. "Bismarck Sea." *Washington Post*. September 4, 1945, Pages 2-4.

Milner, Simoel. *Victory in Papua*. Office of Chief of Military History, Department of the Army, Washington, D.C., 1957.

———. *U.S. Army Forces in World War II*. Vol. II. Cartwheel, the Reduction of Rabaul. Office of Chief of Military History, Department of the Army, Washington, D.C., 1959.

Morison, Samuel Eliot. *History of the U.S. Navy Operations in World War II*. Vol. I. Breaking the Bismarck Barrier. Boston: Little Brown & Co., 1963.

———. *The Two Ocean War*. Boston: Little Brown & Co., 1963.

NATIONAL ARCHIVES—Records and Manuscripts Section, Washington, D.C.

ADVON 5th Air Force Report, Port Moresby, New Guinea, 6 April 1943

Air Unit History, 5th Air Force
  3rd Bomb Group
  35th Fighter Group
  38th Bomb Group
  43rd Bomb Group
  49th Fighter Group
  90th Bomb Group (321st Squadron)

ATIS REPORTS (Allied Translator and Interpreter Section of Japanese Reports)

  Adachi Operation Order
  Bismarck Sea Operation
  Captured Document of Japanese Naval Officer, #4986
  Eighth Army Operations, JM, pp 55-56, 110
  Eighth Fleet Diary
  Intelligence Summaries: Numbers 68, 1/12/43; 74, 2/27/43; 75, 2/9/43; 77, 2/12/43; 78, 2/16/43; 81, 2/27/43; 95, 17, 4/24/43; and 100, 5/5/43
  Operational Order Supplement, #57
  Operational Order, #157
  Soldier's Diary, part 2, page 63
  Southern Area Naval Operations, JM, pages 48-55

USSB Interrogations:
Numbers 511, 525, 526, 527
Also: Gen, Hatazo Adachi, Lt. Gen. Rimpei Ota, Col. Shoja Ota, Capt. Sodamu Sanagi, Col. Hato Shinohara

General Kenney Reports, pp 142-245, 30 March 1943
CHQ Communication Report, 7 March 1943
JCS (Joint Chiefs of Staff) Reports, Southwest Pacific Area
Air Force Report on Destruction of Convoy in Bismarck Sea, 4 April 1943
Allied Air Force Intelligence Summary, #83, 8 March 1943
Bismarck Sea Action, 28 February—3 March 1943
Tactical Reports of Attacks on Bismarck Sea Convoy, 5 March 1943
United States Strategic Bombing Survey Records
Interrogations on Bismarck Sea Convoy, #485
Interrogation, #511
Interrogation, #572
Questionnaire Responses on Bismarck and Solomon Island, 7 December 1941—9 February 1944

PHOTOGRAPHS
Courtesy of:
3rd Bomb Group History Yearbook
U.S. Army Air Force Photographic Center, Washington, D.C.
U.S. Naval Photographic Center, Naval Station, Washington, D.C.
Captain Rick P. Ducharme, USAF, Magazines and Book Branch, Public Information Division, Office of Information, Department of the Air Force, Washington, D.C.

OPERATION BISMARCK SEA

28 February—4 March 1943

ALLIED UNITS AND PARTICIPANTS

5th Air Force
Dobodura Air Base—3rd Bomb Group, 38th Bomb Group, 49th Fighter Group, 35th Fighter Group
Tufi Air Base—9th Australian Operational Air Group
Port Moresby—43rd Bomb Group, 321st Bomb Squadron (90th Group)

Participants
General Ennis Whitehead, ADVON 5th Air Force Commander, Port Moresby, New Guinea
General George C. Kenney, Commander, 5th Air Force, Brisbane, Australia
General Douglas MacArthur, Commander, Southwest Pacific Allied Forces
Colonel Paul Gunn, Chief of Service Command, 5th Air Force
Colonel Bob Strickland, Commander, 3rd Bomb Group
Major Ed Larner, Commanding Officer, 90th Bomb Squadron, 3rd Bomb Group

Colonel Bob Morrissey, Commander, 49th Fighter Group
Colonel Richard Legg, Commander, 35th Fighter Group
Colonel Roger Ramey, Commander, 43rd Bomb Group
Colonel Fay Upthegarde, Commander, 38th Bomb Group

Army Units
Australian Kanga Force, Wau, New Guinea

JAPANESE UNITS AND PARTICIPANTS

8th Area Headquarters, Rabaul, New Britain
8th Fleet, Rabaul
11th Air Fleet, Rabaul
7th Air Division, New Guinea
7th Fighter Command, New Guinea
18th Army, New Guinea
51st Infantry Division
102nd Infantry Brigade
77th Infantry Brigade

Lae Supply Convoy
Cruisers: *Shirayuki* (flag of convoy) and *Tenryu*
Destroyers: *Arishio, Tokotsukaze, Asashio, Yukikaze, Uranami, Shikanami, Hatsuyuki, Asagumo*
Troop Transport Marus: *Nojima, Kyoikusei, Oigawa, Teiyo, Nichiryu, Myoko*
Freighter Marus: *Schichisei, Kamo, Gisha, Kambu*
Tankers: two unnamed

Participants:
Admiral Masatomi Kimura, Commander of Lae Resupply Convoy
Captain Yukata Tishayuna, Executive Officer of Lae Resupply Convoy
Captain Yusi Watanabe, Security Chief of Lae Resupply Convoy
General Hitoshi Imamura, Commander-in-Chief, 8th Area Japanese Forces, Rabaul
General Hatazo Adachi, Commander, 18th Army, New Guinea

General Toru Okabe, Commander, 102nd Brigade, Rabaul and New Guinea

General Sata Nakano, Commander, 51st Japanese Infantry Division

Admiral Gunichi Mikawa, Commander, 8th Outer Sea Fleet, Rabaul

Admiral Jinichi Kasaka, Commander, 11th Air Fleet, Rabaul

General Rimpei Ota, Commander, 7th Air Division, New Guinea

Colonel Hato Shinohara, Commander, 7th Fighter Command, New Guinea

Allied Air Bases: Port Moresby, Tufi, Dobodura, and Wau, New Guinea

Japanese Air Bases: Lae, Madang, and Wewak, New Guinea; Gasmata, Cape Gloucester, and Rabaul, New Britain